hamlyn

Choosing Childcare

Discover what's right for you
and your child

Ruth Edensor

I would like to dedicate this book to my children Natalie and Daniel and to my husband Mark for their love and support. With special thanks to Mum and Dad.

NOTE

Information in this book is believed to be correct at the time of going to press, but the publishers cannot be held responsible for errors and omissions. Readers are advised to check for the most up-to-date information with their local Children's Information Service (see Useful Contacts on pages 138–139 for details).

A Pyramid Paperback

First published in Great Britain in 2006 by
Hamlyn, a division of Octopus Publishing Group Ltd
2–4 Heron Quays, London E14 4JP

ISBN-13: 978-0-600-61458-6
ISBN-10: 0-600-61458-1

A CIP catalogue record for this book is available from the British Library

Printed and bound in China

10 9 8 7 6 5 4 3 2 1

Contents

Introduction

Choosing childcare is one of the most important – and most difficult – decisions a parent has to make because it has such an enormous impact on how children develop. Good quality childcare has a positive impact on everything from a child's self-esteem to his eventual career path. But how do you get it right? This book has been written to help parents who are undecided about what type of childcare is best for their child and their family's needs.

What the book is about

With more childcare options available than ever, selecting the right one for you can be daunting, especially for first-time parents. This book is designed to help you by setting out all the different types of childcare out there. It explains all the choices on offer inside your home, from nannies and mother's helps to au pairs. It also looks at the full range of care options outside the home, such as children's centres, day nurseries, playgroups and crèches. An overview of each type of childcare outlines what it has to offer, detailing the hours of care, age range catered for, staffing ratios and how much you'll have to pay. The book explores the pros and cons of using each type of care, and looks at how your child might feel in different care settings.

If you decide to opt for childcare in your own home, the book explains how to choose and where to find a home childcarer to suit your circumstances, then looks at what to expect from her and how to ensure a good relationship develops between you all. Childcarers are referred to as 'she' throughout because most carers are women, but men can make excellent providers. To help you make an informed decision on childcare facilities away from home, there are check lists of things to look for and lists of questions to ask when visiting a childminder or nursery. You'll learn how to assess the indoor and outdoor facilities – are they safe, age-appropriate, stimulating, clean and plentiful? – and how to judge the atmosphere – is it calm and friendly, are the children playing well and how do staff interact with their charges? The book specifies the kinds of activities you should expect your child to be doing, and looks at the importance of structured routines and planning.

What makes a good childcare worker? Just because someone works in the field of childcare and has a relevant qualification doesn't mean she's going to be great at her job. Inevitably, some childcare workers are better than others; as in any kind of job, some are just more dedicated and conscientious, and go that bit further to ensure your child is cared for in a way that meets all her emotional and developmental needs. To help you make the right choice, the book explores what's best for children of every age and personality type. And, of course, what's best for every type of parent, too.

Advice on everyday practicalities

Making your choice of carer is not the end of the process. In order to settle your child into her new surroundings or get her accustomed to her new home carer as tearlessly as possible, it helps to prepare her well and establish a goodbye routine. The book contains tried-and-tested techniques that help children adjust and quickly start enjoying time away from you. There is advice, too, on successful ways to communicate with your childcare provider, keeping your relationship sweet long-term ensures the best possible care for your child. Once your child has settled into the new routine, you'll want to be reassured not only that she is flourishing, developing confidence and an enthusiasm for learning, but that she is safe from abuse and neglect. The book details signs of both: although you are unlikely ever to need them, it is always comforting to have that knowledge. You may find that after your child has settled into a new childcare arrangement her behaviour changes slightly as she tests new boundaries. She'll need firm guidelines from you in order to feel secure. Letting her get away with things because you feel guilty about leaving only increases a child's anxiety; this issue, too, the book explores in detail.

When you need to move on

As a parent, you will want to keep an eye on your child's care and review it as she grows. If she has been with a childminder since babyhood, for example, you might want to introduce more formal provision and some mixing with other children to prepare your child for school. Or your own circumstances and childcare needs may change. Simply look at the book again to help pinpoint the right type of childcare for you and your child at every new life stage.

The importance of quality childcare

Children learn from the actions of their parents and carers, and from the environment surrounding them. And so if we want children to be healthy, happy, well-adjusted and to reach their full potential, we need to provide them with a loving, predictable environment in which to develop. Unfortunately, children can sometimes be exposed to childcare that is not high enough in quality. Although that this is rare, it can happen in any care setting – and in the home, too. The effects of three different styles of childcare environment are set out below. They range from one extreme – strict – to the other – lenient – and sometimes overlap if care is inconsistent. A balance in the middle – consistent, loving and positive – is best for children's development and is the one to keep in mind when seeking high quality childcare.

A strict environment

In this type of care children are rarely given freedom to choose what they do. Carers are critical of children's actions and tend to highlight negative behaviour, giving little praise or recognition when children behave well or achieve something good. They may use negative forms of behaviour management, such as belittling, shouting and even smacking. People who adopt this style of childcare often expect perfection from children. This sort of environment may help children conform, but at what price?

THE EFFECTS

Children growing up in an authoritarian environment generally become:
- Angry.
- Rebellious.
- Forgetful.
- Submissive.
- Nervous.
- Frightened.
- Indecisive.
- Introverted.

A lenient environment

Lenient childcarers may let children do anything for a quiet life. They probably ignore misbehaviour, make few demands on children, have scarce rules and little structure to the day. Carers may exercise little or no control over children and let them choose their own schedule, including when they go to bed or when and what they eat. Lenient carers set low standards and generally tolerate immature behaviour from children, giving into whining, nagging and crying.

THE EFFECTS

Children growing up in a lenient environment generally become:
- Insecure and low in self-esteem.
- Lacking in a concept of right or wrong.
- Aggressive and lacking in self-control.
- Domineering.
- Disinterested in reaching goals.

A positive environment

A well-balanced, positive environment allows children the freedom to explore, become independent, confident and develop their skills. In this type of atmosphere adults supervise children well, yet make sure they know the boundaries by establishing clear rules. They keep expectations realistic and set out consistent consequences for misbehaviour, while children are given lots of positive attention and praise when they try hard and for good behaviour. Children's energies are carefully channelled into positive learning activities, and this safe, stimulating and loving environment motivates a child's natural curiosity and promotes all areas of learning, building positive attributes and strong relationships between carers or parents and children.

THE EFFECTS

Children growing up in a positive environment generally become:

- Active and outgoing.
- Independent.
- Positive.
- Self-controlled.
- Sociable and friendly.
- Confident.
- Cooperative.
- Able to express their needs.
- Aware of others' needs.
- Able to manage their feelings.
- Responsible for their actions.
- Full of initiative.
- Able to reach their full potential in education.

Assessing your needs

Everyone is different, with a particular set of circumstances, whether domestic, work-related, family or financial. The type of childcare that suits one person and their child may not be right for another. Even children within the same family have different needs. It is important to take time and consider all the options available to you.

The charts on the following pages will help you to work out what your practical needs are – full- or part-time care, for instance – and which type of childcare best suits these requirements. Scan across the top line to check which needs you have to meet, then run down the columns to find out which types of care are most appropriate for you. To help whittle down the contenders make a note of likely choices, then read up on each one by turning to the pages indicated.

CHILDCARE AT HOME

	Full-time	Part-time	Hours available	Average cost	Age range	Free places for 3–4 year olds	Registered and inspected	Term-time only	Family support	Open all year	For details see
Nanny/home childcarer	yes	yes	flexible	£2.50–£4.50 per hour per child	all	no	no	no	no	no	pages 21–25
Maternity nurse	yes	yes	24 hours	£700 per week	babies	no	no	no	yes	yes	pages 26–28
Au pair	no	yes	varies	£50 per week	all	no	no	no	no	yes	pages 28–31
Mother's help	yes	yes	varies	£60–£150 per week	all	no	no	no	no	no	pages 31–33
Babysitter	no	yes	flexible	£3.50–£5 per hour	all	no	no	no	no	no	pages 33–36
Grandparent/ relative	yes	yes	flexible	varies	all	no	no	no	yes	yes	pages 36–39
Leaving children home alone	no	yes	flexible	none	see pages 32–33	no	no	no	no	yes	pages 39–40

CHILDCARE OUTSIDE THE HOME

	Full-time	Part-time	Hours available	Average cost	Age range	Free places for 3–4 year olds	Registered and inspected	Term-time only	Family support	Open all year	For details see
Childminder	yes	yes	varies	£2.50 per hour	0–8	no	yes	no	no	yes	pages 49–53
Day nursery	yes	yes	7.30 am–6 pm	£133–£144 per week	0–5	yes	yes	no	no	yes	pages 54–56
Children's centre	yes	yes	7.30 am–6.30 pm	£140–£195 per week	0–5	yes	yes	no	yes	yes	pages 57–60
Local authority nursery	yes	yes	8 am–6 pm	varies	0–5	yes	yes	no	yes	yes	pages 61–63
Neighbour-hood nursery	yes	yes	8 am–6 pm	£140–£195 per week	0–5	yes	yes	no	possible	yes	pages 63–65
Early Excellence Centre	yes	yes	8 am–6 pm	£140–£195 per week	0–5	yes	yes	no	yes	yes	pages 66–68
Work-place/ college nursery	yes	yes	8 am–6 pm	£140–£195 per week	0–5	yes	yes	no	no	varies	pages 68–70
Montessori nursery	yes	yes	8 am–6 pm	£850–£1,300 per term	0–5	yes	yes	no	no	yes	pages 71–73

	Full-time	Part-time	Hours available	Average cost	Age range	Free places for 3–4 year olds	Registered and inspected	Term-time only	Family support	Open all year	For details see
Nursery school	yes	yes	9 am–3.30 pm	varies	3–4	yes	yes	yes	no	no	pages 74–76
Playgroup/ parent and toddler group	no	yes	am and pm sessions	£1.50–£5 per session	0–5	yes	yes	yes	no	no	pages 77–80
Sure Start activity	no	yes	varies	mostly free	0–4	yes	yes	no	yes	yes	pages 80–83
Crèche	no	yes	varies	£3–£5 per session	0–8	varies	see pages 72–73	no	no	no	pages 83–85
Out-of-school care	no	yes	varies	£7 per session/ £75 per week	3–11	no 74–75	yes	see pages	no	no	pages 86–88
Overnight care	no	yes	6 pm–8 am	varies	3–16	no	see pages 76–77	no	no	no	pages 89–91

Finding financial assistance

Childcare can be very expensive, but help with the costs is available from a variety of sources, and nine out of ten families are eligible for Child Tax Credit. Here is everything you need to know about the options.

Child Tax Credit

Provided that the combined income of you and your partner (if you have one) falls below a certain threshold, if you have a child under the age of one, you can benefit from Child Tax Credit, whether you are working or not. Money is paid into the bank account of the main carer.

Working Tax Credit

This tax credit allowance offers help with childcare costs for parents on low incomes who are working. Up to 80 per cent of childcare costs can be claimed back. The credit takes into account the annual salary of you and your partner (if you have one) and money is added directly to your PAYE pay cheque or paid into your bank account if you are self-employed. To qualify for help with funding you must be using an approved home carer, registered childminder, nursery, play scheme or out-of-school club. The Tax Credits helpline can help you fill in forms or check the progress of an application (see Useful Contacts on page 138 for details).

THE CHILDCARE ELEMENT

To apply for Working Tax Credit families must:

- Use registered or approved childcare.
- Work more than 16 hours per week (in a two-parent family, both parents must work more than 16 hours; lone parents must work over 16 hours and partners of a parent who is incapacitated must also work more than 16 hours).

Free childcare for three and four year olds

Local authorities, funded by the government, provide free part-time early education places for all three and four year olds. Children may attend a total of five two-hour sessions per week at a registered and inspected facility for 11 weeks per term. The number of sessions may change and is likely to increase; your childcarer will keep you informed, or contact the Early Years Department of your local authority.

All children are entitled to a total of six terms of free childcare by the time they are of school-entry age, which is the term after they turn five.

When to start claiming

Child's birthday	Free place available
1 April–31 August	Autumn term following 3rd birthday
1 September–31 December	Spring term following 3rd birthday
1 January–31 March	Summer term following 3rd birthday

Childcare subsidies

Some employers subsidize childcare places, perhaps by £5 or so per day, paying the childcare provider directly. Other employers might offer childcare vouchers for the childcare provider to redeem. Universities and colleges may offer discounted fees of up to 50 per cent to staff and students. Teenage mothers in full- and part-time education, including Modern Apprenticeships, can apply for the costs of registered childcare under the Care To Learn? scheme (see Useful Contacts on page 138 for details).

Care for children with special needs

All registered childcare providers are required to be aware that some children have special needs, perhaps a physical disability or a particular educational requirement. To promote the welfare and development of such children, it's important that their childcare providers work as a team with you, the parent, and all the relevant agencies.

Children with disabilities

Years ago, children with disabilities such as cerebral palsy, Down's syndrome, or impaired sight or hearing attended special schools. Now, they increasingly join mainstream education at the early years stage. Children who have physical disabilities are likely to have had a support team of professionals and carers from an early age and, as a parent, you probably know a great deal about the problems your child faces. When considering childcare it is important to take advice from your support team and to look for a place that has an ethos of inclusion throughout the facility so your child feels part of the group.

Children with special educational needs

The term 'special educational needs' encompasses many different problems, from moderate learning difficulties with reading, writing, spelling and numeracy to speech delay, behavioural challenges and conditions including dyslexia, dyspraxia, dysphasia, dyscalculia and autistic-spectrum disorders. Often parents are first to sense that something is holding a child back from achieving or working to his or her best ability. If you feel something might be wrong, it's essential that you take responsibility for making sure your child gets appropriate care and extra support as early as possible. This helps minimize any frustration and development delay. When some children start childcare, neither parents nor carers are aware that they have a special need. The child may be too young for a difficulty to have manifested, or the problem might not have been spotted. But once you have a diagnosis, try to find out as much as possible about the difficulty by speaking to a Special Educational Needs (SEN) adviser at the place of childcare. By the time children with special needs reach school age, or before if appropriate, they may be offered extra help by the SEN adviser, either in small groups or one-to-one.

What childcarers have to do

In order to become registered, childcare providers have to meet the following requirements for children with special needs:

- Make available to parents a written statement about special needs consistent with the code of practice for the identification and assessment of special needs.
- Be able to adequately meet the needs of every child in their care.
- Make the physical environment suitable for a child with physical difficulties, as far as is reasonable.
- Ask parents whether they should liaise with other agencies about care and equipment the child needs, and ensure those needs are met as fully as possible.
- Consider the privacy of a child with special needs during their care.

If you need help

When you are not satisfied with the level of support you are getting or would like more information, ask an SEN adviser to help you get in touch with the Early Years Department of your local authority or with relevant special needs support groups.

Chapter 1

Childcare at home

When you start the process of choosing the right type of childcare for you, your child and your family, it's best to consider all the options available, both in your home and outside it. Once you've given thought to everything available in your area, you'll be in a better position to make an informed decision. The very best childcare choice is the one that makes both you and your child feel happiest. Deciding that you would like your child to be looked after at home leads you to the next step: choosing a carer. Whether you opt for a nanny, au pair, mother's help or relative to look after your child obviously depends on the hours you need to cover, the age and personality of your child, and what level of care you require – there are different options for full day care and short time slots throughout the day. All the alternatives are explored in this chapter, with information on what to expect from each, how much they cost and where to start your search.

Pros and cons of childcare at home

Parents often choose to have someone care for their child in their own home in the belief that children are safer and more secure in a familiar environment. Some maintain that staying at home all day means less disruption for the child and makes it more likely that the carer will give children more undivided attention. It certainly makes leaving home for work in the morning that much easier. But as with all types of childcare, it has pitfalls that you need to contemplate before making the decision about which type of care is right or wrong for you. Some pros and cons you might like to consider are set out below:

ADVANTAGES OF HOME CARE

- Children experience little disruption to their daily routine.
- No travel required to deliver and collect children from care centres.
- Care is less formal than in day-care facilities.
- Children receive individual care and attention tailored to their specific needs.
- Siblings can stay together.
- Children have more freedom to eat and drink when and what they like.
- Shy children can be more confident in familiar surroundings.
- You have more say about a child's routines and rules than in nurseries.
- Easier to make visits to or receive visits from the extended family.
- If you work from home you can see your children more often.

POTENTIAL DISADVANTAGES

- The work involved in hiring a carer, such as a nanny, and being her boss.
- Can be the most expensive form of childcare, involving extra household expenditure and possibly agency fees, insurance and travel expenses.
- Many childcarers who work in the home have no childcare qualifications.
- If the childcarer is ill you are left without cover.
- Holiday arrangements can be a source of conflict.
- Loss of privacy with another adult in the home, possibly living in.
- Increased wear and tear on the home.
- Children get close to a carer and can be upset when she leaves; the close relationship may make some parents feel envious or jealous.

What is a nanny?

Trained nannies can offer high quality, professional childcare in your own home. Untrained nannies may need supervision and you'll have to assess their skills unaided. On the following pages you will find everything you need to know, from what nannies do to where to find one and how to check out her qualifications.

Type of care	Full- or part-time at home
Age range	All ages
Hours of care	A full-time nanny works around 40 hours per week
Qualifications	None required, but often have a childcare qualification
Regulatory body	None, unless registered as a home childcarer through the Childcare Approval Scheme (see pages 51–52); The Department for Trade and Industry has revised regulations for nanny agencies to reassure parents that staff are vetted properly
Police check	Not required unless you are registering with a childcare approval scheme. But you can do this yourself, with the approval of the nanny
Approximate cost	£2.50–£4.50 per hour per child; £16,000–£27,000 per year

What a nanny does

- Takes sole charge of children for the day (if required) while you are in or out of the house.
- Provides nutritionally balanced meals for your child, as advised by you and according to your choice of diet.
- Has responsibility for all aspects of care and children's wellbeing.
- Provides stimulating, age-appropriate play to encourage children's development.
- Takes children to school and to extra-curricular activities, including making lunch boxes and ensuring children have equipment and kit ready.
- Cleans and maintains children's toys, rooms and clothes.

Qualifications

A nanny does not have to be qualified, but many are trained in childcare and look for a nanny position as a first job fresh out of college. While they may be perfectly able to do the job, nannies coming straight from college tend not to stay in their first job for long, and some move on because they do not like the experience. Some nannies have lots of experience but no qualifications; your ideal nanny has both. It's wise to give careful consideration to a nanny who has neither qualifications nor experience.

- Children receive individual care and attention in their own home, which minimizes disruption to life.
- Children build a close relationship with one other carer.
- You don't have to run children to nursery before starting work.
- It reduces your workload.
- Often fits into your life more flexibly than day care.
- Siblings can stay together instead of being in different childcare facilities.
- Help during school holidays and in picking up children from school.

- An expensive form of childcare.
- There is no government requirement for registration or checking of nannies, although they can take part in the Childcare Approval Scheme (see pages 51–52).
- Nannies do not have to be qualified or experienced.
- A nanny fresh out of college has no real life experience of the job.
- You don't really know what the nanny gets up to during the day.
- May reduce your privacy, especially if the nanny lives in.
- Some nannies feel homesick and do not settle.
- Having a disagreement with a nanny can make home life awkward.
- You must take out employer's and public liability insurance, make sure your home contents insurance contains an endorsement for the nanny, and that you update your motor insurance if you wish her to use your car.
- The nanny should have public liability insurance.

Types of nanny

Once you have decided that you are interested in employing a nanny, start to think about the different types of nannies out there. Although each one undertakes the same sort of tasks as outlined above, they work different hours and may live in or out of your home, depending on your family's needs.

1 The daily nanny

A daily nanny lives in her own home and comes to your home every day. This is a good idea for parents who have a structured day, for instance those who work from nine to five and know when they will be in and out of the house.

THE PROS

- A great choice if you do not have a spare room in which to accommodate a nanny.
- You have more privacy if a nanny is not living with you.
- Your relationship may feel more professional if the nanny does not live in.
- Hours of work are clearly set out, so you both know where you stand.
- You may feel less responsible for a nanny who leads an independent life.

THE CONS

- The nanny is not readily available in the evening or early mornings.
- You have to rely on the nanny to be punctual.
- She may move to another job if her living arrangements change.
- Wages are higher than for live-in nannies.
- Parents who work outside the house might not get much time to catch up on the nanny's news at the end of the day.

2 The live-in nanny

If you need to be flexible with your childcare, for instance if your work is unpredictable and involves late nights or early mornings, a live-in nanny is an ideal way to enable your children to stay at home. You also benefit from having an extra pair of hands around the house.

THE PROS

- You can agree the nanny's hours, day or night, to suit your needs.
- You have plenty of time to discuss the children and any other issues.
- Can be good company for a parent who spends long periods of time alone.
- Someone is home for the children from early morning until late at night.
- Children have individual care tailored to their own needs.
- Siblings can stay at home together.
- Babysitting can be pre-arranged for evenings out.

- Loss of privacy.
- Can be the most expensive form of childcare, since you also have to cover expenses such as heating and food.
- Some nannies may be homesick.
- You have to give up a spare room for the nanny.
- A bad atmosphere may develop between you if you disagree on how to handle issues such as behaviour.
- You may not like the nanny's habits.

3 The shared nanny

You may like to share a nanny with a friend to cut the costs and allow your children to mix with others. Discuss whether to alternate time spent in each house or to stay at one base. The nanny may live in one of the houses or live out, with the disadvantages and advantages as detailed above. Spend time drawing up an agreement between the two families, spelling out day-to-day duties and the division of costs. Many families find it simpler for the nanny to live out and then split both the costs and time spent in each house down the middle.

4 The home childcarer

If a nanny working in England looks after more than two families in the home of one of the children cared for she must register as a childminder or home childcarer with the Childcare Approval Scheme. This scheme provides recognized national status for individuals who provide childcare in a child's own home. For more information see pages 51–52.

Who can use a nanny?

Anyone who can afford it and can give up a spare room if the nanny lives in.

What's on offer for children with special needs?

A nanny can be a great help in caring for a child with special needs because she gives one-to-one care that meets specific requirements in the home, where any specialist equipment is at hand. An extra pair of hands at home can be particularly helpful if your child has mobility problems.

The cost of a nanny

Costs vary greatly and depend on how many children the nanny is looking after. The following figures are approximate per annum and subject to change:

Daily nanny From £18,000 in rural areas to £27,000 in London
Live-in nanny From £16,000 in rural areas to £20,000 in London
Shared nanny As above, but shared with the other family
Home childcarer As a childminder, see pages 49–53

How to find a nanny

- Word-of-mouth recommendation.

- Nanny agencies.

- Your local Children's Information Service (CIS).

- *The Lady*, *Nursery World* and other parenting and childcare magazines.

- An internet search.

- Advertisements (or by advertising) in local newspapers.

THE CHILD'S POINT OF VIEW

Children can gain a great deal from having a close relationship with a good nanny, including enjoying all the advantages of being at home with one regular carer. If the relationship develops well, children can be looked after with the minimum of disruption to everyone's life and you'll be assured that they are happy and thriving.

SEE ALSO **What's best for your child?**, pages 114–116; **What's best for you?**, pages 116–118; **What makes a good childcare worker?**, pages 118–120; **Conducting an interview**, pages 42–45; **Choosing the right home carer**, pages 40–42; **Getting the best from your carer**, pages 45–46.

What is a maternity nurse?

The early days of parenthood can be a wonderful time; they are also a time when new parents are crying out for extra support. Maternity nurses are trained and experienced nannies or nurses who have qualified to work with newborn babies. They are employed on a short-term basis following childbirth and are primarily responsible for the care of a mother and her newborn baby. Self-employed, maternity nurses can help out five or six days a week for 24 hours a day or for a few days or nights only depending on the parents' needs. While most maternity nurses are willing to take on extra duties, it is essential to discuss tasks such as looking after siblings and general household cleaning at the interview and before making a booking.

Type of care	Full-time or part-time, but short-term after childbirth
Age range	Newborn babies
Hours of care	On call six days a week 24 hours a day, with time off in between
Qualifications	Usually qualified in childcare and/or neonatal nursing
Regulatory body	None
Police check	Not required, but you can do this yourself, with the approval of the nurse
Approximate cost	£600–£1,000 per week

What a maternity nurse does

- Provides support and guidance to parents on all aspects of caring for a newborn baby, including establishing feeding and sleeping routines, and advising on common concerns and ailments.

- Advises on breast-feeding.

- Makes up bottle feeds and sterilizes equipment and can bottle-feed the baby day or night.

- Bathes and changes the baby.

- Keeps the nursery clean and tidy.

- Washes and irons baby clothes and looks after equipment.

- Takes over completely for a while.

- Extra duties may include: preparing family meals, walking the dog, shopping, caring for siblings.

Qualifications

Agencies require that a maternity nurse is qualified in childcare and has at least two years' post-qualification experience working with babies aged up to 12 months. In addition, she may be qualified as a Registered Health Visitor or Registered Sick Children's Nurse, Registered Nurse, Advanced Neonatal Nurse Practitioner or Advanced Baby Practitioner.

ADVANTAGES OF USING A MATERNITY NURSE

- Offers invaluable help with essential chores at a time of upheaval.
- Ensures the new mother and father have time and confidence to enjoy and bond with the baby.
- Replaces the support of the extended family in the newborn period when this is not available or desirable.
- Especially helpful for multiple births or for long recoveries after surgery.

POTENTIAL DISADVANTAGES

- Very costly.
- Mothers who feel protective and want space and time alone with the baby might find a maternity nurse an intrusion.
- You might feel the maternity nurse is taking over (though a good practitioner takes this into consideration).

Who can use a maternity nurse?

Available to parents of newborn babies who can afford the expense.

What's on offer for children with special needs?

A maternity nurse only usually focuses on newborns. If your infant has any special needs, she may be a source of support, comfort, reassurance and advice on the best way to care for your baby.

The cost of a maternity nurse

Costs vary but you can expect to pay approximately the following per week, which excludes travel expenses:

One baby £600–£700
Twins £700–£800
Triplets £900–£1,000

How to find a maternity nurse
- Word-of-mouth recommendation.
- Agencies (usually a dedicated service within nanny agencies).
- Resource lists from local home birth and natural childbirth support groups.

SEE ALSO **What makes a good childcare worker?**, pages 118–120; **Conducting an interview**, pages 42–45; **Choosing the right home carer**, pages 40–42; **Getting the best from your home carer**, pages 45–46.

What is an au pair?

An au pair working in the United Kingdom is a single person between the ages of 17 and 27 who has come to study English and works for up to five hours a day in the home. A good au pair is adaptable, flexible and likes children. Many parents find them invaluable and they become part of the family. Au pairs can be particularly effective in bilingual families, where parents would like children to grow up immersed in the mother tongue. Agencies can help you select your au pair and may offer a three- or four-week trial period.

Type of care	Part-time under your supervision
Age range	All ages
Hours of care	Between 15 and 35–40 hours per week
Qualifications	None required
Regulatory body	None, however the Foreign Office offers guidelines
Police check	Not required
Approximate cost	£50 per week

What an au pair does
- Helps with household chores.
- Washing, ironing and simple cooking.
- Looks after children for short periods supervised by you.
- Babysits for one or two evenings per week.

Qualifications
Au pairs do not have to be qualified, but it's obviously an advantage if they have some experience looking after children, such as younger siblings.

QUALIFYING FOR THE FOREIGN OFFICE AU PAIR SCHEME

The Foreign Office's au pair scheme offers guidelines on the employment of au pairs in the UK and a list of countries that qualify. Both may change at any time, so your prospective au pair must check with the British High Commission or the British Embassy in her own country before travelling. Countries that qualify: Andorra, Bosnia-Herzegovina, Republic of Bulgaria, Croatia, Faroe Islands, Greenland, Macedonia, Monaco, Romania, San Marino, Turkey. European Economic Area (EEA) and Swiss nationals are allowed to come to the UK as au pairs but aren't included in the scheme. For full, up-to-date guidelines contact the British High Commission (see Useful Contacts on page 138).

VISA REQUIREMENTS

Nationals of some countries need entry clearance or a visa to enter the UK. The British High Commission can give full details on who needs to apply and how (see above). Entry requirements for au pairs change from time to time, but current guidelines state that au pairs must:

- Stay no longer than two years.
- Want to study English.
- Show they will leave the country after the two-year period.
- Prove they will not apply for government aid, such as income support, while in the UK.

ADVANTAGES OF USING AN AU PAIR

- Useful for older children who no longer need a full-time nanny.
- You have a resident babysitter who can be called upon at short notice.
- Offers an extra pair of helping hands around the house.
- Can be good company, if you want it.

POTENTIAL DISADVANTAGES

- Not suitable for full-time sole care of children.
- Because au pairs come from abroad it is difficult to meet before the arrangement starts, which can make the settling-in period difficult.
- Unlikely to have qualifications in childcare.
- Not registered or checked by childcare agencies.

- Lack of privacy if a young stranger lives in your home and joins in the daily routine.
- It costs £50 per week, plus board.
- You must give up a spare room for the au pair.
- Lack of good English can lead to communication difficulties.
- Time off to attend English classes might not suit your family's schedule.
- Homesickness may be a problem.
- May not be able to handle tough situations, such as children's behavioural or first-aid needs.

Types of au pair

There are three types of au pair. They all live in your home.

1 The demi au pair

Works three days a week for 15 hours and babysits for one or two nights a week.

2 The working au pair

Works five days a week for 25 hours and babysits for one or two nights a week.

3 The au pair plus

Works five to seven days a week for 26–35 hours and babysits for one or two nights a week.

Who can use an au pair?

Available to all who can afford the cost and have space in the home.

What's on offer for children with special needs?

Au pairs may be able to help you care for your child, depending on the severity of the child's needs and the au pair's experience. However, most au pairs will need to be under your supervision and guidance at all times.

The cost of an au pair

Au pairs charge approximately £50 per week; on top of this you cover their full board and lodging in your home. An au pair needs her own room. After the first six-month period of work, it is customary to give an au pair two weeks' paid holiday leave.

Demi au pair £15 per week plus living expenses

Working au pair £50 per week plus living expenses

Au pair plus £65–£80 per week plus living expenses

How to find an au pair

- Word-of-mouth recommendation.

- Au-pair agencies: try searching the internet or local telephone directories.

- Your local Children's Information Service (CIS).

- *The Lady*, *Nursery World* and other parenting and childcare magazines.

SEE ALSO **What's best for your child?**, pages 114–116; **What's best for you?**, pages 116–118; **Conducting an interview**, pages 42–45; **Getting the best from your home carer**, pages 45–46.

What is a mother's help?

As the name suggests, a mother's help assists a mother (or father) with childcare and household chores. She usually lives in with the family. A mother's help is often a young adult with little childcare experience and is rather like an inexperienced nanny. Because of her age and experience, a mother's help works under the direct supervision of parents, but as you gain confidence in her abilities you may wish to give her more responsibility; even sole charge of the children eventually. Mother's helps can live in or away.

Type of care	Full-time or part-time, usually under your supervision
Age range	All ages
Hours of care	Maximum 45 hours per week
Qualifications	None required
Regulatory body	None
Police check	Not required, but you can do this yourself, with the approval of the mother's help
Approximate cost	£60–£150 per week

What a mother's help does

- Helps parents with the daily routine of caring for children.

- Plays with the children.

- Washing and ironing.

- Light housework (most households with a mother's help also employ a cleaner).

- Assists with shopping and cooking.

- Up to two nights' babysitting per week.

Qualifications

A mother's help does not need any qualifications because she works in the family home alongside a parent. You may be able to find a mother's help who is interested in studying for a childcare qualification part-time at the same time as working.

ADVANTAGES OF USING A MOTHER'S HELP

- It's like having an extra pair of hands and may help you find more time to spend with your children.
- Children may grow fond of her; socializing with another adult can give them confidence.
- Can be good company if you are home alone for long periods.

POTENTIAL DISADVANTAGES

- Not suitable for full-time sole care of children.
- Unlikely to have qualifications in childcare.
- Not registered or checked by the government.
- May not do things around the house as you would like them done.
- May have conflicting ideas about behaviour management.
- You share your home with another adult.
- The expense can be off-putting.
- May need emotional support if young or away from home.
- May not be able to handle tough situations, such as children's behavioural or first-aid needs.

Who can use a mother's help?

Available to all who can afford the cost and can give up a spare room if she is to live in.

What's on offer for children with special needs?

A mother's help can be very useful if you have a child with special needs in that she gets on with household chores, such as cooking and cleaning, while you look after your child. Depending on the severity of the child's special needs and the arrangements you have with your mother's help, she may also be able to help provide some care, under supervision.

The cost of a mother's help

Costs vary, but wages start at approximately £60 per week for an inexperienced 16 year old rising to around £150 per week for a more experienced, older mother's help. Take into account also the cost of board and lodging if the mother's help is living in. She should be given two days off per week, taken to suit you and the family but usually at the weekend. She also takes off every evening except the two set aside for babysitting. A mother's help who lives out usually works Monday to Friday and expects a little more money.

How to find a mother's help

- Word-of-mouth recommendation (the best option).
- Agencies: try searching the internet or local telephone directories.
- Try your local Children's Information Service (CIS).

SEE ALSO **What's best for your child?**, pages 114–116; **What's best for you?**, pages 116–118; **Conducting an interview**, pages 42–45; **Getting the best from your home carer**, pages 45–46.

What is a babysitter?

Babysitters come from varied backgrounds and it is important to choose one who is able to cope with the demands of the job. A sitter looking after a baby who is asleep will have to anticipate feeding, changing and playing with the infant. If looking after toddlers who may be asleep when she turns up, the sitter should make sure she gets to know the children at another time of day before starting the job. When using a teenage babysitter, get to know her better first by chatting with the parents and don't forget to set some ground rules on bed time routines and what children can (and can't) eat and drink, play or watch.

Type of care	Part-time for short periods
Age range	All ages
Hours of care	Negotiable
Qualifications	None required
Regulatory body	None
Police check	Not required, but you can do this yourself, with the approval of the babysitter
Approximate cost	£3.50–£5 per hour

What a babysitter does
- Takes charge of children for a short time only.
- Gives children undivided attention.
- Checks every half-hour to see that the children are fine.
- Closely supervises children who are not in bed to make sure they are safe and happy.
- Makes time to do fun things with children, such as playing board games and reading stories.
- Follows the parent's bed time routine.
- Optional tasks: a responsible babysitter might like to earn extra money when children are asleep doing chores such as ironing.

Qualifications
Babysitters do not have to be qualified, although it is a bonus if they do have some experience looking after younger brothers and sisters.

ADVANTAGES OF USING A BABYSITTER

- Gives you a chance to recharge your batteries and get out of the house for a short time.
- Allows couples to spend time out together.
- With a live-in childcare worker care can be seamless.
- If children enjoy the babysitter's company it builds their social skills, which boosts self-esteem.
- Some grandparents enjoy being given responsibility for children without any parental involvement.
- An overnight carer from a nanny agency can be a lifesaver when you have a newborn and need to catch up on sleep for a few nights.

POTENTIAL DISADVANTAGES

- Unlikely to have qualifications in childcare or be registered.
- You must arrange for non-drivers to be picked up and dropped home. If you intend to use a taxi, make sure the sitter is comfortable with the idea.
- If you use a babysitter under the age of 16 you remain responsible for your child when you are out of the house (see pages 39–40).

- Shy children might not be comfortable with a sitter; lively children might not be well-enough behaved.

Who can use a babysitter?
Available to all who can afford the expense.

What's on offer for children with special needs?
Many babysitters are young with little experience, so consider carefully your child's needs and the sitter's abilities before booking one. If you manage to match up the child's needs with the babysitter's experience, sitters can be very helpful, giving you a break for short periods. Babysitting agencies may have on their books more mature people with experience of dealing with your child's special needs.

The cost of a babysitter
Babysitters charge around £3.50–£5 per hour; however you can pay a great deal more, especially if you use an agency or live in London. Come to an agreement before employing the sitter to prevent any discord on the evening, making sure you discuss rates for parts of an hour, after midnight and at peak times, such as Saturday night, New Year's Eve and Christmas Eve. Pay in cash on your return home.

How to find a babysitter
- Word-of-mouth recommendation (the best option).
- Local colleges that offer childcare courses: students can make great sitters and have been police-checked. Telephone the tutors and ask to be put in contact with interested students.
- Your local Children's Information Service (CIS) may hold lists of sitters.
- Search for babysitting agencies on the internet or in local telephone directories.
- Advertisements (or by advertising) in *The Lady*, *Nursery World* and local parenting and childcare magazines.
- Join or set up a babysitting circle or do swaps with friends for free.

SEE ALSO **What makes a good childcare worker?**, pages 118–120; **Conducting an interview**, pages 42–45; **Choosing the right home carer**, pages 40–42; **Getting the best from your home carer**, pages 45–46.

Why use a relative as carer?

Many parents choose to put their career on hold or work part-time around their partner's hours so that they can care for their children themselves at home. More and more fathers whose partners earn a good wage are choosing to be a stay-at-home dad, or house husband. Other parents involve children's grandparents or other relatives closely in their day-to-day care. If you feel torn between having to go to work and wanting to stay at home with children, remember that the most important thing you can do for your children is to be happy. If you are unhappy leaving a stimulating career you worked hard to achieve and become an unhappy parent stuck at home your children may pay the price. Children can also tell if you are miserable leaving them every day in day care so you can go back to work. Only getting the balance right for you can make it all work well.

Type of care	Full-time or part-time
Age range	All ages
Hours of care	Negotiable
Qualifications	None required
Regulatory body	None
Police check	Not required, but you should not use anyone you don't trust absolutely
Approximate cost	Varies, but similar to a local childminder (see pages 49–53)

- Witnessing the children's milestones.
- You stay in charge of all aspects of childcare, including discipline, routines and activities.
- Looking after children can be very rewarding.
- You are with your children, not worrying about what they are doing while you are at work.
- Some parents fit studying or self-employment around childcare.
- You are there to look after the children when they are ill.

POTENTIAL DISADVANTAGES

- You don't get paid.
- It's not the easy option; parenting can be hard work and monotonous.
- Children's behaviour can be challenging and overwhelming at times.
- You might miss adult company.
- Isolation can be an issue, especially for fathers – often activities for children are attended mostly by women.
- It can be difficult to keep children occupied all day, every day, especially if money is tight and during the winter when you need to stay in more.
- You often don't get a break day or night.

INFORMAL ARRANGEMENTS

Many parents, particularly of school-aged children, work out a system of childcare swaps with friends, taking it in turns to look after each other's children for short, unpaid sessions. This can be especially useful after school or during the holidays. Be aware that if the care is on a regular basis for more than two hours the carer must be registered as a childminder, unless children are looked after in their own home.

Using grandparents or relatives as carers

As many as one in ten grandparents are thought to look after their own grandchildren regularly. If you are considering having your parent or other close family member look after your children, it is important to consider whether they are physically fit and capable of doing the job and, if they are using their own home, whether it is safe.

Qualifications

Relatives used as carers don't have to be qualified, although it is a bonus if they have some experience of looking after children.

ADVANTAGES OF USING GRANDPARENTS OR RELATIVES

- They love your child and your child loves them; being together often only strengthens this bond.
- Usually very cheap and often free of charge.
- They may live locally.
- Flexible timing; many grandparents are able to adapt to your timetable.
- School and nursery pick-ups are usually covered.
- Relatives often look after the children when they are ill.
- Other children can come to play.
- If care takes place in the child's own home, toys and equipment are to hand and the space can be child-proofed.

POTENTIAL DISADVANTAGES

- Unlikely to have qualifications in childcare or be registered.
- If elderly, grandparents may find looking after young children very tiring.
- You may have conflicting ideas about discipline and other childcare issues.
- It may be difficult to discuss worries and other issues because of your relationship with the relative.
- A grandparent's or relative's house may not be as child-proof as yours.
- Grandparents or relatives may not feel at ease attending activities such as tumble tots or swimming lessons.

The costs

Having a relative look after your child can be one of the cheapest forms of childcare. If you are paying for the care you might like to negotiate a rate similar to the amount you would pay a local childminder. Your carer needs to be registered for you to be able to claim tax credit.

What's on offer for children with special needs?

If they are willing, grandparents can be a wonderful source of help in caring for a child with special needs. They often have a great deal of up-to-date knowledge about the child's abilities and progress, as well as access to specialist toys and equipment. Above all, they have lots of love to give.

SEE ALSO **Choosing the right home carer**, pages 40–42; **Getting the best from your carer**, pages 45–46.

Leaving children home alone

The dilemma of when a child is old enough to be left at home alone has to be faced by most parents at some point and can be a daily predicament for those who work long hours. Despite public and professional concerns about the subject, no laws state when it is safe to leave your child at home unsupervised. If a child beneath the age of 16 were put at risk emotionally or physically while left on his own, Social Services staff might regard it as neglect, a form of abuse. Depending on the severity and circumstances of the case, the child might be entered on a Child Protection register until circumstances change. You are the best judge as to whether your children can cope on their own and for how long. Think about it honestly: the following guidelines might help you consider the circumstances:

What to consider before leaving a child

- The age of the child: the NSPCC (National Society for the Prevention of Cruelty to Children) considers most children under the age of 13 too young to be left on their own for more than a short period, and children under the age of 16 too young to be left alone at night.
- How responsible the child is and her level of understanding.
- The amount of time the child is left: you should never leave a baby or young child unsupervised, asleep or awake, even for a short time.
- How often you leave your child.
- Where she is left and how safe the environment is.
- Whether other children are left in the home and how old and mature they are.

Action plan before leaving home

- Make sure children are confident and happy to be left alone.

- Leave your contact number and other trusted people's numbers.

- Leave the house safe by locking away items such as medicine and tools.

- Talk to children about dangers in the home: not putting knives in the toaster, touching electrical items with wet hands, for example.

- Explain to children what to do in an emergency, such as getting out of the house, calling emergency services and not opening doors if they suspect a fire.

- Show children where the basic first-aid kit is and what to do with it.

- State when you will return and stick to it or ring if you will be late (a great example to give children when they start going out alone).

- On returning, ask how they got on; talk about what may have troubled them and what they enjoyed.

SEE ALSO **What's best for your child?**, pages 114–116; **What's best for you?**, pages 116–118.

THE CHILD'S POINT OF VIEW

How your children feel being left alone depends very much on the circumstance and their personalities. If a child is not really ready to be left, even for a short time, because he is too young and immature, he is likely to feel anxious, scared and lonely, and perhaps even rejected and panicky. Children who are prepared to be left alone for a short time and who are mature enough to cope are likely to enjoy the responsibility and it may help raise their self-esteem.

Choosing the right home carer

Whichever type of carer you think might provide the best care in your home, mother's help or nanny, au pair or grandparent, and whatever qualifications and experience they have, the most successful will share similar personal qualities. The personality traits that mark people out as natural childcarers are set out below, together with ways of judging them on paper and when you meet face-to-face. There are more details on pages 118–120.

Personal qualities to look for

1 Positive outlook
People with a sunny approach to life project this quality in their work. They tend to handle children using positive strategies, such as praising good behaviour. This helps children feel good about themselves and raises their self-esteem.

2 Calm demeanour
A carer who can be calm in stressful situations will be able to take charge and not escalate problems.

3 Communication skills
Good communicators explain difficult tasks to children by breaking them down into manageable chunks. They clearly ask children to do things, rather than telling them what not to do. They chat to you about what has gone on during the day – achievements as well as problems. Good communication with children encourages language development and speech plays a major role in learning.

4 Initiative
Being able to handle unexpected situations that crop up is essential. Someone who can see what needs doing without being asked and gets on with the job makes your life easier in the long run. Different types of carer are left on their own with children in different measures, and this affects how much initiative they need. A nanny in sole charge needs to use initiative throughout the day to make it run smoothly, while an au pair might never be left alone with a baby (though you still want her to use initiative with household chores). However, remember that initiative has to be balanced with respect for your wishes.

5 Time-management skills
People who can manage time well are organized with children's routines, get children where they need to be on time, and plan out interesting days.

6 Love of children
Needless to say it is a good idea to choose a carer who enjoys the company of children. With love of children comes an urge to bring out the best in them.

7 Trustworthy and honest
It is important to have a carer that you can trust your children with.

8 Diplomatic and confidential

It is essential for your carer to be diplomatic and keep family issues confidential.

Assessing qualifications

Someone who has studied for a recognized childcare qualification will have an understanding of children's needs at different ages. She is obviously interested in children or would not have spent time training in this field. If you are contemplating taking on a recently qualified student you might like to talk to her course tutor to learn more about her personal qualities. See page 119 for details of childcare qualifications and pages 106–107 to find out who inspects and registers your childcarer.

Assessing experience

Just because someone has the right qualifications doesn't mean she is a great nanny or maternity nurse. Someone with years of experience and no formal qualifications may be more suitable for a post because she knows more about what the job entails and has proven that she enjoys caring as a career. You can gain great insight from references from previous jobs, so do take them up; call previous employers for a chat if you have outstanding queries or concerns.

Making the choice

Try to give equal weight to your potential carer's personal qualities, level of experiences and qualifications in order to gain a clear picture of whether you think she is the right person for the job. Ideally you would be able to employ someone with all the personal qualities detailed above, as well as appropriate qualifications and some hands-on experience of the job. Failing that tall order, you may find someone with experience who would like to study to gain qualifications or someone who is qualified and eager to gain practical experience. It is important to follow your instinct and pick someone you feel will really care for your children and fit into your home life.

Conducting an interview

Interviewing face-to-face is essential if you are to pick the right person for the job, and it is helpful to have several candidates to choose from. Do interview potential carers yourself, even if they have come through an agency: there's no better way to assess how compatible you are. Ideally, your partner would be at the interview, too, to add his or her thoughts. This is especially important if you are all going to share a bathroom and kitchen. Alternatively, a friend might help you conduct the interview and is sure to have useful impressions of candidates.

What to do before the interview

- Make a list of duties you expect the carer to carry out.

- Decide on the hours you would like the carer to work, including when the day starts and ends. If you need her to get up to a baby in the night, consider when in the day the carer can catch up on rest.

- Determine the salary and holiday entitlement.

- Think about whether you need the carer to accompany you on holidays at home and abroad.

- Set some house rules, such as use of telephone and online time, inviting in friends and boyfriends, where the carer takes meals and spends evenings.

- Think about whether the interview should be formal or relaxed.

- Plan the structure of the interview: when to show candidates the house, when to explain the job, where to sit, for example.

- Work out when to introduce the children.

Points to consider during the interview

1 Do candidates want the job?

It is possible that candidates just need any job and not really this one. You will be able to tell if people are really interested in the job by the way they interact with you, their questions, and their tone of voice. Also note whether they ask about your children and if they are receptive to them when they meet.

2 Will they fit in?

You need a carer who fits in with your family and is a team player. A good team player communicates well, keeps to commitments, is clear about what is expected of her and what she wants. She's also honest and reliable, diplomatic and keeps matters confidential. Very importantly, she has a common goal in mind – the welfare of your child. As the employer, you are also part of the team, and need to show the same qualities to keep the home happy. Getting to know a carer as well as you can before you make a job offer helps you decide if she really is a good team player. You can only do this by interviewing, taking up references, spending time together and, importantly, by following your instinct.

3 Will they do a good job?

Judge whether each candidate could give your child the best possible care by considering the qualities that make a good carer (see pages 41–42).

Questions to ask

These questions are guidelines only and are directed at interviewing a nanny. Adapt them to fit the childcare worker you are interviewing. An interview with a babysitter need not be quite as formal.

- What experience do you have working with children?
- What training and qualifications, including First Aid, do you have?
- What do you like most about looking after children?
- Why did you (or why are you) leaving your last job?
- Why do you want to be a nanny?
- What do you think are the qualities of a good nanny?
- Are you willing to undertake all the duties in the job description? Is there anything you would not like to do?
- Which activities do you like doing with children?
- What kind of things would you do with the children during the day?
- Can you give an example of a daily routine you would set up for my children?
- How would you act if the children misbehaved? Give an example.
- Tell me about a difficult situation you have had at work and how you resolved it.
- How would you cope in a medical emergency?
- What sort of hobbies and interests do you have?

What to do after the interview

Follow up your chosen candidates' references, asking previous employers about each carer's duties in the job, reliability, sickness record, and strong and weak points. You will also need to see certificates to check on qualifications (it is a good idea to ask potential carers to bring them to the interview); check them against the lists of relevant qualifications on page 119. Make your choice by considering all the answers given in the interview and the results of the references, but, most importantly, follow your gut instinct, choosing someone you feel is right for your family and who will bring out the best in your children.

CANDIDATES FROM ABROAD

It may not be feasible to interview candidates who come from overseas. If you hire through an agency, the staff will have vetted the candidate for suitability and will try to match you with someone they feel fits your requirements. However, you should still obtain references and speak to the candidate on the telephone several times. If you feel you like the sound of the person, ask them to come for a trial period of around three to four weeks. Better still, but more unusually, you might pay for your potential carer to come over for a short visit.

Getting the best from your home carer

Choosing to have childcare in your own home means you become somebody's manager. Although nannies and au pairs are unlikely to be as formal as to call you their boss, if you see yourself as one you can start to think about what it takes to manage staff well and so get the best from your childcarer. Being a parent is hard work: not only do you have to run your house and balance the demands of your partner, children and job, you now have to take care of the carer. It can be a difficult juggling act, but applying some of the people-management skills below might help smooth over times of conflict.

Ten ways to get the best from your carer

1 Employ the right person
It's hard to get the best out of someone who doesn't really want the job and it will be impossible if the person does not like children, so making sure you choose the right carer is vitally important.

2 Create a happy environment
As in any job, with a happy atmosphere, nice environment and good benefits employees work better and have more job satisfaction.

3 Communicate well

Without good communication between you and the carer you won't get the best from her. If she knows exactly what she needs to do, she is more likely to be able to do it; being left guessing can make her feel uncomfortable and do the wrong things.

4 Appreciate your carer

Let her know when you are pleased with her work; it will make her feel appreciated, which in turn encourages her to give her best more consistently.

5 Be friendly and approachable

Your carer should feel she can come to you for help in resolving problems.

6 Be interested in your carer as a person

If you show interest in your carer's life and in her as a person and not just as an employee you will make her feel you care, which makes her happier in her work.

7 Spend time with your carer

If you are trying to build up a relationship with your carer nothing beats spending time together and possibly doing something fun. If you don't feel you have time for an 'activity', just chatting over a drink can help.

8 Be assertive

Let a carer know when you would like her to do something differently. If you ask with respect she's much more likely to be happy to change her ways. If you put carers down and humiliate them when they make an error they are likely to feel resentful and less likely to please.

9 Be democratic

Discussing plans and giving a carer choices about what she does encourages cooperation and job satisfaction. Simple choices are good; try, 'Would you like to take the children to the park or go swimming today?'

10 Train carers to do a good job

An inexperienced carer may need you to be hands on, showing just how you like your cooking and ironing. Even experienced nannies may need help and direction getting a colicky baby to sleep. Being involved and helping out is the best way to improve a carer's skills.

Chapter 2

Childcare outside the home

The many options for childcare outside the home are explored in this chapter: nurseries of every type, playgroups and crèches, childminders and school-based clubs. Reading up on the advantages and the drawbacks of each form of care outside the home may help you decide whether this arrangement will suit you better than having someone care for your child at home. Make the right decision now and the care will be all the better for being a lasting and sustainable solution to your needs and those of your child.

Pros and cons of childcare away from home

Although there are many advantages to using childcare outside the home, there are many aspects that may not be ideal. If you cannot find the perfect solution (and as with all types of childcare, perfect is all-but impossible), you may have to compromise on a few things. You may, for instance, have to travel further than you would like, take time off work if your child is ill (day-care centres do not care for sick children) and come to terms with your child not getting out and about as much as you would like. But there's one thing you must never compromise on: the quality of care your child receives. Here's how.

ADVANTAGES OF OUTSIDE CARE

- You gain time and space away from your children.
- A system of government checks works to ensure children have access to high quality care and an early-years curriculum.
- Your child spends time with other children of the same age if you choose a nursery.
- One of the cheapest forms of childcare, especially if you take advantage of playgroups and free childcare places for three and four year olds.
- Reliability: nursery and playgroup colleagues cover for each other during times of sickness and holiday leave.
- Constant care: day nurseries, some children's centres and childminders offer childcare for up to 48–51 weeks a year and from babyhood to age five.
- A wide range of toys, equipment and activities are available for children.
- Children interact with staff and other children from a variety of backgrounds, helping develop their social skills.
- Children get used to formal care, which prepares them for school.
- Trained staff can offer advice on child development and parenting issues.

POTENTIAL DISADVANTAGES

- You may not see your children as much as you would like.
- You may feel excluded from the care of your child if you need childcare for long periods of time (see Staying Involved, page 133).
- Your child may have to be away from home for many hours each day.

- Your child may simply not want to go on some occasions, which can be stressful for you both.
- If you work, you may need to take time off if your child is ill: sick children cannot attend childcare outside the home.
- It can be difficult to find high quality childcare for babies outside the home.
- You may sometimes be unhappy with the way situations are handled.
- Children will not have as many opportunities to see extended family or other friends as they might like.
- High staff turnover in nurseries can be common.
- Siblings of different ages will most likely be cared for in different rooms in nurseries.
- Trips outside the facility may not be as frequent as you would like.
- You do not have a say in choosing staff unless you use a childminder or parent-run playgroup.

What is a childminder?

Childminders are self-employed and work mostly or all of the time from their own home. They look after other people's children for more than two hours a day and are a popular choice for childcare, especially if you work shifts or don't need a nine-to-five service. Trust your instincts when choosing a childminder (see page 51 for types of childminder); although registered minders are strictly regulated, the best choice for you will be someone who shares your values and parenting style and is willing to adapt to your child's daily routine.

Type of care	Full-time or part-time
Age range	0–8 years (12 in Scotland)
Hours of care	Flexible; may work outside regular hours
Qualifications	None required, but see page 50
Registered and inspected	Yes (see page 106), plus police-checked
Approximate cost	£2.50 per hour per child

What a childminder does
- Takes sole charge of children in her own home.
- Provides nutritious meals, snacks and drinks throughout the day, unless you arrange to provide a packed lunch.

- Offers toys appropriate to a child's age and stage of development.
- May take older children to and from school.
- Sometimes looks after additional older children in the school holidays.
- Follows government guidelines for registered childminders.

Qualifications

Childminders do not have to be qualified in childcare, however registered childminders are expected to attend a pre-registration briefing session and a first-aid course. The local authority offers training in subjects such as child protection, which can improve a minder's skills. If a childminder you are considering has completed these types of courses it shows she is interested in and committed to a career in childcare.

Carer to child ratios

Age of child	Carer	Number of children (including minder's own)
Under 5 years	1	3 children; only one under 12 months
Under 8 years	1	6 children

4 year olds attending 10 childcare sessions per week may be classed as over 5 years

Special circumstances More than one child under 12 months or more than three under fives may be accepted for a short period only; triplets are accepted together.

ADVANTAGES OF USING A CHILDMINDER

- Often a very flexible service; minders may be willing to take children outside normal day-care hours.
- A less expensive childcare option.
- Often close to home, which cuts down on travelling time.
- Homely environment: your child becomes part of another family.
- Children can be given individual attention.
- Care can be adapted to meet each child's sleep patterns and feeding times.
- Continuity of care: children can stay with a minder until they start school.
- You get to know the childminder and her family and may become good friends.
- Siblings can be cared for together (in a large nursery they may be split up).
- Sleepovers or weekend care might be possible.
- Minders often have good links with local playgroups and toddler groups.

- No strict timetable: minders can go out if a child is energetic or stay in if tired.
- May pick up older brothers and sisters for pre- and after-school care.

POTENTIAL DISADVANTAGES

- Illness may leave you without childcare at short notice.
- The age mix of children minded may not suit your child.
- You may not really know what goes on during the day, or how the minder occupies your child.
- The minder might not share your approach to parenting issues, such as discipline, junk food and spending time outdoors (see Staying Involved, page 133).

Types of childminder

Once you have decided that a childminder is the way to go for your family, start to think about the different types of minder you might employ.

1 The registered childminder

Childminders who look after children under the age of eight (12 in Scotland) are required to be registered and inspected by the relevant regulating bodies in different parts of the UK (see pages 106–107). In order to become registered, childminders are inspected to ensure that their home is safe and suitable for the care of children and that they fulfil the guidelines used in that country. They and anyone else over the age of 16 years living in the house are police-checked.

2 The unregistered childminder

Childminders do not have to be registered if: they are the child's parent, foster parent or close relative; if care is given wholly or mostly in the child's own home; if the childminder looks after children for two sets of parents wholly or mainly in the home of either or both sets of parents; or if they care for children between 6 pm and 2 am. If minders aren't registered when they should be they could be prosecuted.

The Childcare Approval Scheme carer

Through Sure Start (see pages 80–83), the Department for Education and Skills (DfES) has developed this registration scheme for carers working in England. It may be adopted in the rest of the United Kingdom in the future. The scheme allows previously unregistered childcarers working in the child's home, such as nannies, the chance to gain recognized national status. Childcarers who work with children over seven years of age and/or on other domestic premises are also eligible to register. A carer may have an NVQ Level 3 qualification in childcare (see page 119) if she works alone with children. Many nanny agencies only accept nannies who are qualified to this level. As an alternative, she should have attended childcare induction and first-aid courses.

THE PROS

- You know the carer is over 18 years old and qualified to look after children.
- Working parents may be able to access financial support through the Working Tax Credit scheme, childcare vouchers or employer-supported care (see pages 16–17).
- Carers are police-checked with the CRB (Criminal Records Bureau) and POCA (Protection of Children Act 1999).
- Carers have a valid pediatric first-aid certificate.
- The carer's work-place has been inspected.
- Carers have completed a health check.

THE CONS

- The carer's certificate of registration is valid for one year only, so you must ask to see it and check the date.
- The scheme does not state which age group carers are suitable for: for reassurance, take up references and consider experience.

Who can use a childminder?

Anyone who can afford one.

What's on offer for children with special needs?

Gauge how suitable a minder might be for your child by the interest she shows in his abilities (rather than disabilities), routines, likes and dislikes. If your child has severe disabilities, think seriously about whether the minder has the facilities to care for him. The minder will need to be able to identify your child's needs, then make sure she can meet them. You can help her do this by thinking about the questions opposite. It's important to keep communicating closely throughout your relationship to prevent difficulties and monitor progress.

- Will you adapt activities so my child can join in?
- Do you have all the specialist equipment you need or can we lend you some?
- How will you encourage my child to feel positive about himself?

The cost of a childminder

Using a childminder can be one of the cheapest forms of childcare. Fees vary considerably, but tend to range between £1.70 and £3 per hour per child; often much more in greater London. Some childminders may give a reduction for a sibling. Check what a minder considers to be extra hours for which she may charge a different rate and also what charges are made for late pick-ups. Allow also for hidden expenses, such as providing nappies and milk formula or ready-made bottles for a baby, and for funding trips out.

How to find a childminder

- Word-of-mouth recommendation.
- The National Childminding Association (see Useful Contacts on page 138).
- The Early Years Department of your local education authority.
- Your local Children's Information Service (CIS).
- Advertisements (or by advertising) in local newspapers.
- Advice from your health visitor.

THE CHILD'S POINT OF VIEW

Children who have a childminder can benefit from spending days in a homely environment with a small number of other children and familiar adults. The ideal childminder's home becomes an extension of the child's own home; in its warm, friendly atmosphere your child should feel secure and confident.

SEE ALSO **What's best for your child?**, pages 114–116; **What's best for you?**, pages 116–118; **What makes a good childcare worker?**, pages 118–120; **Choosing the right home carer**, pages 40–42; **Getting the best from your home carer**, pages 45–46.

What is a day nursery?

A day nursery offers more than four hours of continuous care and education for the under-fives and is a good option if both parents need reliable, full-time childcare and like the idea of their child being with others in a group setting. A day nursery may be private, charitable or state provided. For different types of nursery, see also pages 57–76.

Type of care	Full-time or part-time
Age range	6 weeks–5 years; after-school or holiday care may be available up to 8 years
Hours of care	7.30 am–6 pm, sometimes longer
Registered and inspected	Yes
Approximate cost	£133–£144 per week

What a day nursery does

• Provides full day care throughout the year for children under eight (school-age children may be cared for before and after school and during holidays).

• Follows early years curriculum planning, encouraging each child to reach his or her potential in areas of learning set out in the Birth to Three Matters framework and the Foundation Stage Curriculum for three to five year olds (see pages 104–106).

• Offers stimulating play opportunities that promote a child's all-round development.

• Prepares and provides nutritious meals, drinks and snacks throughout the day.

• Provides an age-appropriate environment to support development and learning through play.

• Monitors a child's achievements.

• Follows guidelines for registration and inspection by providing a safe, stimulating and clean environment.

Staff and qualifications

The manager is responsible for managing staff and overseeing the care and welfare of all children in the nursery. She also ensures that facilities such as rooms and equipment are properly maintained. At least half the staff must be qualified in childcare up to Level 2 or above (for qualification details see pages 118–119). Supervisors and managers must be qualified to at least Level 3 in childcare.

Minimum staff to child ratios

Age of child	Staff	Number of children
0–2 years	1	3
2 year olds	1	4
3–7 years	1	8

At least two staff must be on duty at all times. In a room there should be no more than 26 children in any group, depending on the room size. Babies (under 2s) must not be cared for in groups of more than 12. Day nursery sizes vary enormously from small concerns attached to or in residential homes to purpose-built nurseries for around 100 children.

ADVANTAGES OF USING A DAY NURSERY

- Open for up to 12 hours a day.
- Reliable service available 50 weeks or more of the year, five days a week.
- Usually accepts babies, so children can be cared for in a familiar place for some years if they start young.
- Children benefit from socialization and integrated care and early education.
- Qualified and experienced staff, lots of well-planned activities and a wide range of toys.

POTENTIAL DISADVANTAGES

- Siblings of different ages are cared for in different rooms (some parents might consider this an advantage).
- May be some distance from your home.
- If the nursery is outside the catchment area for your child's school it may take more effort for your child to meet up with friends once at school.

Who can use a day nursery?

Private day nurseries are open to anyone. Other nurseries may have certain restrictions on who can use them (see individual entries on pages 57–76).

What's on offer for children with special needs?

As with other forms of registered childcare, the manager and staff must be aware that some children have special needs and include them in activities as far as reasonably possible. Staffing ratios may be upped to meet the needs of disabled children, with fees adjusted accordingly.

Opening times

Usually 8 am till 6 pm, sometiimes later, Monday to Friday, 50 or more weeks of the year.

The cost of a day nursery

Costs vary, but are approximately £144 per week for 0–2 year olds, £133 per week for 2–5 year olds. Costs are higher in some parts of London compared with other parts of the country. All meals are usually included: check with individual nurseries. There may be hidden expenses, such as providing nappies and milk formula or ready-made bottles for a baby. Most nurseries charge extra (around an hour's fee) for each 15 minutes you are late in picking up children. There may be a booking fee and a minimum number of sessions you must sign up for. A number of free sessions per week are available for three and four year olds (for details see pages 16–17).

How to find a day nursery

- Word-of-mouth recommendation.
- Your local Children's Information Service (CIS).
- Contact the National Day Nurseries Association (see Useful Contacts, page 139).
- Local telephone directories.
- An internet search.
- Noticeboards at local primary schools, libraries, playgroups, baby clinics and GP surgeries, local children's clothes shops and baby-friendly cafes.

SEE ALSO **What's best for your child?**, pages 114–116; **What's best for you?**, pages 116–118; **What makes a good childcare worker?**, pages 118–120; **What makes a good childcare facility?**, pages 121–122.

What is a children's centre?

By 2010 the government hopes there will be a children's centre for under fives in every community. A new initiative, these centres are intended to make accessible high quality childcare to parents who need it, integrating care such as early-years education, healthcare, employment advice and support for the family to help provide children with the best possible start in life. You might not have one of these centres in your area yet, and not all the services will be based at the centre itself: some staff will work 'in the community' or your own home.

Type of care	Full-time or part-time day care
Age range	0–5 years
Hours of care	7.30 am–6.30 pm
Registered and inspected	Yes
Approximate cost	£140–£195 per week per child

Free places are available, depending on the child's circumstances. There are also free places for three and four year olds

What a children's centre does

Each children's centre will offer a different combination of services and activities, varying according to the needs of local people, but all will include these basics:

1 Early-years education

Of paramount importance to every children's centre, early-years education starts in the baby room and builds up to more formal but play-based learning for five year olds. Stimulating activities are planned by an education manager who is a teacher with relevant early-years experience. The teacher works alongside nursery staff to ensure each child is encouraged to reach his or her full potential in the areas of learning set out in the national guidelines, such as the Birth to Three Matters framework and the Foundation Stage for three to five year olds (see pages 104–106).

2 Childcare

A care manager is responsible for overseeing the care and welfare of all the children at the centre. She ensures facilities such as nursery rooms and crèches are properly equipped and manages the staff. Staff at these centres are sometimes called 'Educarers' because they provide education and care together.

3 Family support

Some centre staff offer support to families whether they use the day-care facilities or not. Others work specifically with families whose children are looked after at the centre. They provide a wide range of services, with an emphasis on adult education and encouraging parents into work. Staff can steer you toward basic skills and employment advice, parenting courses, for instance on children's behaviour management, and vocational training in childcare. There are also plenty of parent and child activities to promote play and learning. Services may be run by Sure Start staff (see pages 80–83) who are highly experienced in childcare and early-years education. There will usually be a large toy library to borrow from at little or no cost, well stocked with new, high quality toys, and staff at hand to help you choose toys to suit your child's age and stage of development.

TYPES OF SUPPORT OFFERED

- Job Centre Plus to help parents into work.
- Children's Information Service for advice on all local services available to children.
- Library for borrowing books, toys, storytelling and other activities to promote books and reading.
- Home Start support: home visits by volunteers to help identify what help you need and how to get it.

4 Healthcare services

Among the vast array of services on offer at a children's centre pediatric healthcare plays an important role. You can pick and choose which services to use and access many without using the day-care facilities.

HEALTHCARE SUPPORT OFFERED

- Speech and language therapists.
- Health visitors.
- Community nursery nurses.
- Family support workers.
- Physiotherapists.
- School nurses.
- Midwives.
- Children's consultants.

Staff and qualifications

The centre will be run by a centre manager and a care, education and outreach manager. There will also be senior nursery nurses and many staff with childcare qualifications. In addition there is a team of domestic staff, including cleaners and kitchen staff, a caretaker and a bursar.

Minimum staff to child ratios

Age of child	Staff	Number of children
0–2 years	1	3
2–3 years	1	4
4–5 years	1	8

Centres vary greatly and can average around 50 to 110 children, according to the size of the building.

ADVANTAGES OF USING A CHILDREN'S CENTRE

- Many easily accessible services in one building.
- High numbers of experienced and qualified staff.
- Continuity of care, with children staying in the centre from birth to five years (although in different rooms).
- Lots of well-planned activities and new toys and equipment.
- Structured care and routines can benefit children, especially those with behavioural difficulties.
- Children's healthcare professionals on site.
- Your educational and employment opportunities are considered.
- The centre provides activities in the local community.

POTENTIAL DISADVANTAGES

- Centres are large, busy places with many different adults and children in one building.
- Siblings of different ages are separated into different rooms, although they may be able to meet up in the outdoor play area. However, different age groups are often separated outside, too.

Who can use a children's centre?

You must have a child under the age of five, although your child doesn't have to be in day care at the centre for you to access its services. You may need to live within a certain catchment area, for example a Sure Start area (see pages 80–83). Staff will be able to check your status. Pregnant women and their partners can access services such as parent groups and childcare classes.

What's on offer for children with special needs?

These centres are very well equipped to care for children with special needs, especially if sited in new buildings. Many have a wonderful sensory room with the latest equipment – and it is used by all the children. Centres assess each child's individual needs and work with parents and other agencies to ensure the child's welfare and development and offer support to the family, where possible. Children with special needs and physical disabilities play alongside their peers as far as possible, with funding available to employ as many extra support staff as needed to make this happen.

Opening times

Ten hours a day, five days a week for approximately 50 weeks per year. There may be extra activities, such as parenting classes in the evenings and some activities, such as father and child groups, may take place at the weekend.

The cost of a children's centre

Approximately £140–£190 per week for full-time care, depending on your circumstances. Three and four year olds are funded for five short sessions per week during term-time (for details see pages 16–17). The local authority provide a number of free places depending on the circumstances.

How to find a children's centre

- Your local Children's Information Service (CIS).
- The Early Years Department of your local education authority.
- Advice from your health visitor.
- Noticeboards in primary schools and playgroups, baby clinics and GP surgeries.
- Word-of-mouth recommendation.

SEE ALSO **What's best for your child?**, pages 114–116; **What's best for you?**, pages 116–118; **What makes a good childcare worker?**, pages 118–120; **What makes a good childcare facility?**, pages 121–122.

What is a local authority nursery?

Local authority day nurseries offer day-long care for children under the age of five, following the guidelines set down for full-time day care for this age group in your region of the United Kingdom (see pages 104–107). These types of nurseries may also offer services to support families, either on the premises or in your home, and provide information on issues such as child health and development. Eventually, many of these nurseries will be subsumed into a children's centre.

Type of care	Full-time or part-time
Age range	6 weeks–5 years
Hours of care	8 am–6 pm
Registered and inspected	Yes
Approximate cost	Free or subsidized

What a local authority nursery does

- Provides full day care throughout the year for children under five.

- Follows early years curriculum planning.

- Provides play opportunities that promote all-round development.

- Offers nutritious meals, drinks and snacks throughout the day.

- Presents a structured learning environment.

- Groups children by ages in different rooms.

- Monitors and records each child's development.

- Follows guidelines for registration and inspection, providing a safe, stimulating, clean environment.

- Offers free day care for children considered in need, at risk, or on a Child Protection register.

- May take fee-paying children if spaces are available.

- Offers parents support and guidance on parenting and childcare issues.

- May run parents interest group/teenage pregnancy groups or adult education groups.

Staff and qualifications

At least two staff must be on duty and half of the staff need to have a relevant childcare qualification up to Level 2 (for details see pages 118–119). Supervisors are required to hold or be working toward a Level 3 qualification in childcare.

Minimum staff to child ratios

Age of child	Staff	Number of children
0–2 years	1	3
2 year olds	1	4
3–7 years	1	8

There should be no more than 26 children in a room, although there may be more than one room per age group (large nurseries may hold 50 children).

ADVANTAGES OF USING A LOCAL AUTHORITY NURSERY

- Day-long care to suit parents in nine-to-five jobs.
- Staff are trained and experienced in all aspects of childcare and development.
- Children mix with their peers.
- Free or subsidized childcare places help children most in need.
- There is an experienced special needs coordinator.
- You may be offered help and support on healthcare, employment and training.

POTENTIAL DISADVANTAGES

- You must be referred to win a place and there are usually long waiting lists.
- May be far from home, although some families in need are offered free transport.
- Rather formal.

Who can use a local authority nursery?

You need to be referred by your social worker, health visitor, GP or other professional. Priority is given to families in social need and on low incomes, single parents, children who are in need, are disabled or have special educational needs.

What's on offer for children with special needs?

Staff are aware that some children have special needs and strive to make sure they are included in activities where possible and appropriate. Staff should work closely with parents to promote the development of each child and bring in the support of outside agencies, too, if necessary.

Opening times

Hours vary, but tend to be from 8 am to 6 pm. Part-time places for a few mornings, afternoons or full days per week are available; the nursery manager allocates the places.

The cost of a local authority nursery

Places are usually offered free of charge to those in need. Check with each nursery for its policy.

How to find a local authority nursery

- Advice from your health visitor, doctor or social worker.
- Your local Children's Information Service (CIS).
- Local telephone directories.
- Local Early Years Department.

SEE ALSO **What's best for your child?**, pages 114–116; **What's best for you?**, pages 116–118; **What makes a good childcare worker?**, pages 118–120; **What makes a good childcare facility?**, pages 121–122.

What is a neighbourhood nursery?

The Neighbourhood Nurseries Scheme was introduced by the government to create 45,000 new, good quality, affordable childcare places in the most disadvantaged areas of the United Kingdom. 142 local authorities were eligible for funding to help provide nurseries in the top 20 per cent of areas of deprivation. Funding to set up new nurseries has now ceased, but nurseries that were developed are still offering care, and, along with local Sure Start programmes (with which they might be linked, see pages 80–83), local authority nurseries (see pages 61–63) or Early Excellence Centres (see pages 66–68), they may integrate with the new children's centres (see pages 57–60).

Type of care	Full-time or part-time
Age range	0–5 years
Hours of care	8 am–6 pm
Registered and inspected	Yes
Approximate cost	£140–£195 per week per child

What a neighbourhood nursery does

- Provides full day care throughout the year for children under five.

- May care for school-age children during holidays and before and after school.

- Follows early years curriculum planning.

- Offers play opportunities that promote all-round development.

- Provides nutritious meals, drinks and snacks throughout the day.

- Features a structured learning environment.

- Groups children by ages in different rooms.

- Monitors and records each child's development.

- Follows guidelines for registration and inspection, providing a safe, stimulating, clean environment.

- May provide parent interest groups or training, such as qualifications in childcare (see pages 118–119) or basic skills courses, for which funding may be available.

Staff and qualifications

At least two staff must be on duty at any time and half of the staff need to have gained up to Level 3 in an appropriate childcare qualification (for details see pages 118–119). Supervisors are required to hold a Level 3 qualification in childcare.

Minimum staff to child ratios

Age of child	Staff	Number of children
0–2 years	1	3
2 year olds	1	4
3–7 years	1	8

There should be no more than 26 children in a room, although there may be more than one room per age group (large nurseries may hold 50 children).

ADVANTAGES OF USING A NEIGHBOURHOOD NURSERY

- High quality childcare.

- Children mix with their peers.

- High quality early-years education.

- Qualified and experienced staff are employed, including special educational needs coordinators.

- May offer family support and training.
- A certain number of hours available free for three and four year olds.

POTENTIAL DISADVANTAGES

- It is a relatively expensive form of childcare.
- You may need to travel some distance to find one.
- Care can be quite formal.

Who can use a neighbourhood nursery?

Anyone who can afford the fees and has a nursery in their local area.

What's on offer for children with special needs?

Staff are aware that some children have special needs and strive to make sure they are included in activities where possible and appropriate. Staff should work closely with parents to promote the development of each child and bring in the support of outside agencies, too, if necessary.

Opening times

Hours vary, but tend to be from 8 am to 6 pm, 50 weeks of the year. Part-time places are available; children might be given a place for morning or afternoon sessions, or for a few days a week.

The cost of a neighbourhood nursery

Costs vary, but you should expect to pay approximately £140–£195 per week per child for full-time care. Free sessions for three and four year olds are available (for details see pages 16–17).

How to find a neighbourhood nursery

- Word-of-mouth recommendation.
- The Early Years Department of your local education authority.
- Your local Children's Information Service (CIS).
- Local telephone directories.

SEE ALSO **What's best for your child?**, pages 114–116; **What's best for you?**, pages 116–118; **What makes a good childcare worker?**, pages 118–120; **What makes a good childcare facility?**, pages 121–122.

What is an Early Excellence Centre?

An example of high quality childcare for fives and unders, Early Excellence Centres can be found in rural, inner city and urban areas. Each centre has its own area of expertise and tries to offer support and information for the local community by identifying needs and building on existing childcare provision. Evidence shows that centres have a positive benefit for children and families by reducing family breakdown and helping to include more children with special needs into mainstream school. Along with local authority nurseries (see pages 61–63), neighbourhood nurseries (see pages 63–65) and Sure Start activities (see pages 80–83), Early Excellence Centres may integrate into newly created children's centres (see pages 57–60).

Type of care	Full-time or part-time
Age range	0–5 years
Hours of care	8 am–6 pm
Registered and inspected	Yes
Approximate cost	£140–£195 per week per child

What an Early Excellence Centre does

- High quality early education and day care.

- Family learning and adult education.

- May provide before- and after-school care.

- Offers information to boost parenting skills.

- Outreach support in the home.

- Counselling services.

- Healthcare services.

- Identifies parents' needs and helps them to access services that may help.

- Works with and identifies children with special needs.

- Trains staff and other local early-years providers, such as childminders and carers from the voluntary and private sector.

- Brings together the work of many agencies, such as the local education department and Social Services.

Staff and qualifications

At least two staff must be on duty at any time and half of the staff need to have gained up to Level 2 in an appropriate childcare qualification (for details see pages 118–119). Supervisors are required to hold a Level 3 qualification in childcare. There will be a manager, deputy manager and special needs coordinator.

Minimum staff to child ratios

Age of child	Staff	Number of children
0–2 years	1	3
2 year olds	1	4
3–7 years	1	8

There should be no more than 26 children in a room, although there may be more than one room per age group (large centres may hold 50 children or more).

ADVANTAGES OF USING EARLY EXCELLENCE CENTRES

- High quality childcare.
- Excellent early-years education.
- Many services for the family, from healthcare to adult education.

POTENTIAL DISADVANTAGES

- Care is quite formal.
- Some centres may not take young babies.

Who can use an Early Excellence Centre?

Anyone who can afford the fees and has a nursery in their local area.

What's on offer for children with special needs?

Research shows that these centres have been successful at identifying children with special needs and moving them on into mainstream education at age five.

Opening times

Hours vary, but tend to be from 8 am to 6 pm, 50 weeks of the year. Part-time places are available for morning or afternoon sessions, or for a few days a week.

The cost of an Early Excellence Centre

Costs vary, but expect to pay approximately £140–195 per week per child for full-time care. Free sessions are available for three and four year olds (see pages 16–17).

How to find an Early Excellence Centre

- Word-of-mouth recommendation.
- The Early Years Department of your local education authority.
- Your local Children's Information Service (CIS).
- Local telephone directories.

SEE ALSO **What's best for your child?**, pages 114–116; **What's best for you?**, pages 116–118; **What makes a good childcare worker?**, pages 118–120; **What makes a good childcare facility?**, pages 121–122.

What is a work-place/ college nursery?

A nursery in your work-place, college or university usually provides full day care and therefore follows the same national standards as other day nurseries, with activities and staffing levels replicating those in private and local authority day nurseries (see pages 61–63). If, however, the nursery provides sessional care, in other words less than four continuous hours per day, it will resemble a playgroup much more (see pages 77–80).

Type of care	Full-time or part-time
Age range	0–5 years
Hours of care	8 am–6 pm year-round or during term-time only
Registered and inspected	Yes
Approximate cost	£140–£195 per week per child, before discounts

What a work-place/college nursery does

- Full day care all year or during term-time only for children up to five years.
- Follows early years curriculum planning.
- Provides play opportunities that promote all-round development.
- Offers care for parents at a work-place, university or college.
- May offer spare spaces to children whose parents do not work or study there.
- Prepares nutritious meals, drinks and snacks throughout the day.
- Features a structured learning environment.

- Has different rooms for various age groups.
- Monitors and records each child's developments.
- Follows guidelines for registration and inspection, providing a safe, stimulating, clean environment.

Staff and qualifications

At least 50 per cent of staff must hold a Level 2 qualification in childcare (see pages 118–119) and a minimum of two staff need to be on duty at any time.

Minimum staff to child ratios

Age of child	Staff	Number of children
0–2 years	1	3
2 year olds	1	4
3–7 years	1	8

There must be a maximum of 26 children in one group, but there may be more than one group in the facility.

ADVANTAGES OF USING A WORK-PLACE/COLLEGE NURSERY

- Convenience: taking children to childcare facilities where you work or study may save travelling time.
- Discounted fees of up to 50 per cent may be available to staff and students, especially in universities or colleges.
- With childcare facilities close at hand you can more easily pop in if you want to breast-feed or see your child.
- Often flexible about hours or days of childcare (although there may be a minimum requirement, such as two sessions per week).

POTENTIAL DISADVANTAGES

- Just because childcare is subsidized and convenient does not mean it is the best choice for you and your child.
- You may have to travel with your child on public transport during the rush hour.
- Your child may find it hard to make friends with local children unless your work-place/college is close to home.
- If you work in the nursery as a carer, relationships can be difficult if you have an issue with the care provided.
- You will have to rearrange your childcare when a child reaches school age.

Who can use a work-place/college nursery?

Depending on the nursery, children may be admitted as babies and stay until they are five years old. Priority is usually given to staff or students who work or study in the company or college, although there is likely to be a waiting list.

What's on offer for children with special needs?

All staff will be aware that some children may have special needs, such as a learning or physical disability, and should make provisions for the child's requirements, working alongside the parents and outside agencies if necessary.

Opening times

Times may vary, but full day-care providers are usually open between 8 am and 6 pm. They may open year-round or only during term-time.

The cost of a work-place or college nursery

Costs vary, but are usually similar to other local authority-run full day-care providers at around £140–£195 per week per child. Discounts of up to 50 per cent may be offered to employees or students. There will be free places for three and four year olds for a certain number of sessions per week (see pages 16–17).

How to find a work-place/college nursery

- Word-of-mouth recommendation.
- The Personnel or Human Resources department of your place of work or study should be able to provide details.
- The Early Years Department of your local education authority.
- Your local Children's Information Service (CIS).

SEE ALSO **What's best for your child?**, pages 114–116; **What's best for you?**, pages 116–118; **What makes a good childcare worker?**, pages 118–120; **What makes a good childcare facility?**, pages 121–122.

THE CHILD'S POINT OF VIEW

How children feel about being left in this kind of nursery obviously depends on their age, circumstances and the care they receive. A baby will not notice how near the facility is to you, while older children may enjoy the idea of being close to you, even if they don't see you during the day.

What is a Montessori nursery?

The Montessori teaching method was established by Maria Montessori. Born in 1870, she was the first female physician in Italy and in her medical practice observed and analyzed how children learned. She founded the first 'Children's house' in 1907 and it was there that she developed the Montessori method of education. She believed that if adults can provide the right kind of learning environment for children, then children are self-creating and are able to teach themselves. Private nurseries using the Montessori method are now found the world over, including in many British cities and large towns. Whether small or large, these schools operate according to Maria Montessori's concept that 'The Montessori way is not just a method of teaching, but a philosophy of life'.

Type of care	Full-time or part-time
Age range	3 months–5 years
Hours of care	8 am–6 pm
Registered and inspected	Yes
Approximate cost	£850–£1300 per child per term

What a Montessori nursery does

- Learning focussed: aims to foster competent, responsible, adaptive, life-long learners who can problem-solve for themselves.

- Allows learning to take place in a nurturing, enquiring, cooperative atmosphere.

- Helps children learn through the teacher and through self-initiated experiences.

- Develops children naturally at their own pace to the best of their ability.

- Works on the whole personality of a child.

- Uses a curriculum based on language and literacy, maths, practical life, sensorial and cultural experiences. For example, 0–3 masters and foundation stage.

- Teaches children to respect and care for themselves as well as others, their environment and all other forms of life.

- Holds that children have sensitive periods of development lasting around six years; the 0–6 age group concentrates on development of the senses, which then develops intellect.

Staff and qualifications

There may be a part-time or full-time teacher trained in the Montessori method. At least half the staff have a Level 2 or higher qualification in childcare (for details see pages 118–119). Teachers use observational skills to assess the developmental stages of children, which enables them to plan activities to guide children's learning. Teachers are encouraged to design learning opportunities that promote freedom in a structured environment, so children learn for themselves, and to provide child-centred and child-led activities in a democratic, encouraging and cooperative way.

Staff to child ratios

Age of child	Staff	Number of children
0–2 years	1	3
2 year olds	1	4
3–7 years	1	8

ADVANTAGES OF USING A MONTESSORI NURSERY

- Offers full day-care facilities.
- The Montessori concept encourages the all-round development of a child.
- Montessori materials enable children to learn from their own mistakes and correct them.
- Very effective for children with special needs and gifted children.

POTENTIAL DISADVANTAGES

- An expensive form of care.
- You may have to travel some distance to find a nursery.
- Children who travel outside their local area may find it hard to make close local friends.
- Many other nurseries would say they adopt these methods of teaching without being Montessori-endorsed.
- Care is formal and structured.

Who can use a Montessori nursery?

Open to all who can afford the fees, though there may be a waiting list.

What's on offer for children with special needs?

Montessori schools are highly effective for children with special needs and for gifted children because the learning environment is designed to ensure success for all children. Ask individual nurseries if they can accommodate your child's disability or special needs.

Opening times

A day nursery is usually open from 8 am to 6 pm five days a week, 50 weeks a year. There are full- and part-time places on offer; part-time children attending either morning or afternoon sessions.

The cost of a Montessori nursery

Costs vary, but because Montessori nurseries are privately funded, expect to pay approximately £850–£1,300 per child per term. A number of free sessions may be available for three and four year olds (for details see pages 16–17).

Where to find a Montessori nursery

- Word-of-mouth recommendation.
- Search www.montessorieducationuk.org for your nearest nursery.
- The Early Years Department of your local education authority.
- Your local Children's Information Service (CIS).
- Local telephone directories.
- Advertisements in local children's magazines, clothing shops and baby-friendly cafes.
- Noticeboards at libraries, playgroups, baby clinics and GP surgeries.

SEE ALSO **What's best for your child?**, pages 114–116; **What's best for you?**, pages 116–118; **What makes a good childcare worker?**, pages 118–120; **What makes a good childcare facility?**, pages 121–122.

What is a nursery school?

A variety of childcare facilities describe themselves as nursery schools, which distinguish themselves from other types of childcare facilities because they are overseen by a qualified teacher. An increasing number of primary schools now have a nursery school, often replacing pre-reception classes (which the government ceased to fund in 2005). Whether funded privately or by the government, nursery schools do not accept children until they are over three years of age. If your child has been in a nursery or playgroup you may find the reduced number of staff to children very different. You should think about the school option carefully: just because children are offered a free place at nursery school five mornings a week when they have turned three years old does not mean that it is the best option for such young children.

Type of care	Full-time or part-time (within school hours)
Age range	3–4 years
Hours of care	9 am–3.30 pm
Registered and inspected	Yes
Approximate cost	state schools offer free care; private nursery schools £850–£1,250 per child per term

What a nursery school does

- Provides high quality early years education.
- Provides sessional care for three and four year olds.
- Follows early years foundation stage curriculum.
- Offers a stimulating environment to learn through play.
- Offers a structured learning environment.
- Monitors and records each child's development.
- Follows guidelines for registration and inspection, providing a safe, stimulating, clean environment.

Staff and qualifications

In each class of up to 26 pupils a qualified teacher works with a nursery assistant who holds at least a Level 3 qualification in childcare (see pages 118–119).

Staff to child ratios

Staff	Children
2	26 if the head teacher is not included in the ratio
2	20 if the head teacher is included in the ratio

There must not be more than 26 children in a class, but there may be more than one class on the premises, and they may use the same indoor area and playground.

ADVANTAGES OF USING A NURSERY SCHOOL

- Qualified and experienced staff.
- Children mix with peers who they will start full-time school with.
- Can be an excellent place for children to receive early-years education.
- If the nursery is part of a school, children quickly become familiar with the school environment, routine and staff.

POTENTIAL DISADVANTAGES

- Many three year olds find five sessions a week very tiring, especially if they are afternoon sessions (few nursery schools have sleeping facilities).
- The staff/child ratio is much higher than in other day-care facilities.
- Nursery schools are quite formal and very structured.
- If you work nine to five you will need to find care outside nursery-school sessions.
- May not encourage as much parental interaction as a playgroup.
- Gaining a place in a school nursery does not guarantee a place in the reception class.

Who can attend a nursery school?

Children start nursery school in the September of the school year in which they turn four years old. Therefore, if they are three years old in August they can start nursery in the September of that year. However, different local authorities or private facilities admissions policies may differ. Fill in the application forms when your child reaches two and a half years of age. Over-subscribed nursery schools attached to primary schools may prefer to admit children moving on into the infant school. If there are places available, children out of the school's catchment area may then be offered a place.

What's on offer for children with special needs?

Staff should be aware that some children may have special needs and ensure that they are included in activities where appropriate. In some nursery schools attached to primary schools pupils may be able to use main-school facilities such as sensory rooms and the expertise of experienced special needs coordinators.

Opening times

A nursery school is open during school hours (9 am–3 or 3.30 pm) in the school term.

The cost of a nursery school

The government provides free sessional places for three and four year olds in state schools. Private schools charge approximately £850–£1,250 per child per term. Add in the cost of uniform, PE kits, book bags and other hidden extras.

How to find a nursery school

- Word-of-mouth recommendation.
- The Early Years Department of your local education authority.
- Your local Children's Information Service (CIS).
- Local telephone directories.

SEE ALSO **What's best for your child?**, pages 114–116; **What's best for you?**, pages 116–118; **What makes a good childcare worker?**, pages 118–120; **What makes a good childcare facility?**, pages 121–122.

What is a playgroup? What is a parent and toddler group?

Usually lively, busy places with plenty of activities and a mixed age group, parent and toddler groups offer part-time care and you stay with your child during the session. They're a great way to meet other parents. A playgroup is more structured then a mother and toddler group, offering sessions for children of different ages. Children can start playgroup at around two and a half years of age but they will need to be out of nappies. In playgroup your child may attend three or four short sessions a week on her own, either in the morning or afternoon. Some playgroups are parent-led and you might be expected to help out at one session every couple of weeks on a rota system. You are also encouraged to join the parent committee to make decisions about staffing, fund-raising and the day-to-day running of the group. Parents who work long hours often combine playgroups with childminder care (see pages 49–53) to allow children to mix with peers and experience more formal care for a few hours a week as they near school reception age.

Type of care	Part-time (within school hours)
Age range	0–5 years
Hours of care	Am or pm sessions; not more than five per week per child; term-time only
Registered and inspected	Yes (playgroup only)
Approximate cost	£2.50–£5 per session per child

What a playgroup does

- Provides sessional care, usually morning or afternoon, for children from over two to five years (usually once a child is out of nappies).

- Follows early years curriculum planning.

- Provides play opportunities that promote all-round development.

- Prepares a healthy snack and drinks in the session.

- Offers a structured learning environment.

- Usually based in one room, though different ages may use different sessions.

- Monitors each child's development.

- Follows guidelines for registration and inspection, providing a safe, stimulating, clean environment.

What a parent and toddler group does

- Provides a space where parents can stay while their children mix with other babies and toddlers, rather than a form of childcare.

- Usually meets once or twice a week for a few hours only.

- May be linked to a playgroup.

- Provides an informal place where parents can meet to chat and provide support for each other.

- Offers toys and equipment appropriate for the age and stage of development of children; may be limited in stock.

- May provide healthy snacks and drinks, however parents often provide these.

- May offer a childcare worker to lead singing sessions.

Staff and qualifications

At least 50 per cent of playgroup staff are qualified in childcare to Level 2 or above (for details see pages 118–119). Staff under the age of 17 or qualified to Level 2 or less cannot be left on their own with children. One parent might be on duty on a rota in each session.

Minimum playgroup staff to child ratios

Age of child	Staff	Number of children
Under 2 years	1	3
2 year olds	1	4
3–7 years	1	8

Staff or volunteers include their children in these ratios. Short-term students may not be added to staff ratios. There must be a minimum of two staff on duty at any time. The maximum group size is 26 children, although there may be more than one group on the premises at any one time.

ADVANTAGES OF USING THESE GROUPS

- Very friendly for child and adult alike.

- Parent and toddler groups ease a child into childcare gently because you stay and take part in activities.

- An inexpensive childcare option.

- Children mix with others their own age from their own area.

- At parent and toddler groups you get out of the house and are able to meet other local parents.

- Great if you want to get involved in your child's care and education; playgroups are eager to sign up volunteers.
- Combine well with childminder care; minders often have well-established links to a local group.
- Registered and inspected care.
- You pick up parenting skills from staff and other parents.

POTENTIAL DISADVANTAGES

- Not full-time care; if you work nine-to-five someone will have to pick up your child after the playgroup session and take him to another care facility.
- You have to stay with children who aren't potty trained.
- Closed during school holidays.
- Shy children may feel lost in a large, busy playgroup full of noise and activity.
- Not ideal if you prefer to leave your child and run (these groups usually require some parental involvement).
- Might be rather intimidating for fathers, since this type of group tends to be dominated by women.

Who can attend playgroups/parent and toddler groups?

Parent and toddler groups suit children from early infancy up to the age of two or rising three. Playgroups are for children aged from two or three to school reception age. Children often progress to playgroup from a parent and toddler group on the same site run by the same staff.

What's on offer for children with special needs?

Staff should be aware that some children may have special needs and try as far as reasonable to accommodate them. Children with special needs may attract extra funding that allows groups to take on more staff for one-to-one care, or to train staff appropriately. This extra staffing changes from year to year as children with special needs leave the group.

Opening times

School term-time only. Hours may vary, but tend to be organized in sessions lasting no longer than four hours in any one day and usually around two and a half hours. If groups offer afternoon sessions there must be a break between the sessions with no childcare provided. Morning sessions often start at 9 am and afternoon sessions around 1 pm, ending in time for parents to pick up children at primary school. A playgroup offers sessional care for three or four days per week but with no more than five sessions per week. There may be afternoon and morning groups, with different children attending each.

The cost of a playgroup/parent and toddler group

Costs vary, but these groups are often a cheap childcare option because they are run by parent committees who like to keep session fees low by organizing fundraising events. An average cost is £2.50–£5 per session. You may be charged a fee for each 15 minutes you are late in picking up children or for non-attendance at meetings and rota sessions. There may be an annual booking fee. Free places for three and four year olds may be offered at playgroups (for details see pages 16–17).

How to find a playgroup/parent and toddler group

- Word-of-mouth recommendation.

- Noticeboards at local church halls and leisure centres, baby clinics and GP surgeries, primary schools with nurseries.

- Your local Children's Information Service (CIS).

- Advice from your health visitor.

SEE ALSO **What's best for your child?**, pages 114–116; **What's best for you?**, pages 116–118; **What makes a good childcare worker?**, pages 118–120; **What makes a good childcare facility?**, pages 121–122.

What is Sure Start?

Sure Start is part of the Children Young People and Families Directorate within the department of education and skills. It aims to achieve better outcomes for children, parents and communities by bringing together local agencies and by expanding the availability of childcare, education, family support and healthcare. Sure Start activities are based in a variety of places, such as local schools or public buildings, and some services will move into the new children's Centres as they develop (see pages 57–60). England, Scotland, Wales and Northern Ireland have separate administration for Sure Start but will offer similar services, which will vary from place to place depending on the needs of the area. Outlined here are some common activities and services on offer to families with 0–4 year olds.

Type of care	Parent support and sessional activities
Age range	0–4 years
Hours of care	Staff work 9.30 am–5 pm; occasional evening and weekend sessions
Registered and inspected	Yes
Approximate cost	Free or small charge

What Sure Start does

Provides activities you can do with your child, such as singing, storytelling and tumble tots groups, information on how to access other forms of childcare, and very practical help including, in some areas, free bus passes. The programme is based around the following basics:

1 Early-years education

- Provides high quality early-years education.

- Toy libraries.

- Community-based activities for children to attend with parents, such as children's fitness, baby music, toddler art and creative play classes, and storytelling at libraries.

2 Childcare

- Offers a variety of high quality childcare.

- Crèches are provided during parent activities at community or children's centres.

- Information on local childminders – and support if you want to become one.

3 Family support

- Support for families at home, such as playlink sessions (when a worker brings toys and play ideas to you) and advice on how to access other forms of childcare.

- Behaviour-management courses for parents.

- Fathers' groups.

4 Health services

- Low-cost safety equipment to buy.
- First-aid kits offered free in some areas, as well as vouchers to use at local pharmacies.
- Speech and language therapists.
- Health visitors and community nursery nurses.
- Physiotherapists.
- School nurses.
- Midwives.
- Children's consultants.

Staff and qualifications

A varied team of staff work for Sure Start in each area, including a manager not necessarily qualified in childcare but with skills in a relevant field. A team of office staff arrange trips and activities, handles publicity and promotional materials, and registers families to join the programme. Once you join you can start accessing facilities and activities. A number of qualified childcare workers are attached to each Sure Start area.

ADVANTAGES OF USING SURE START FACILITIES

- Gives you access to a large variety of services for under fives and their families.
- Activities are often free of charge.
- A great way to meet other families with young children in your area.
- A good source of support for families

POTENTIAL DISADVANTAGES

- Age restrictions may apply to some activities.
- Runs in disadvantaged areas only, and even then access is patchy: you may find you are close to a service but are not allowed to use it.
- Children may face a gap between leaving Sure Start activities at four years old and starting school aged around four and a half to five.

Who can use Sure Start?

The programme runs only in demarcated areas of disadvantage with a small percentage of places for people outside the area. If there is a Sure Start scheme near you it may have a catchment area for people who are eligible to join. Services are offered first to those signed up in the catchment area. If there is space you might be able to join a baby music session, for example, even if you have the wrong postcode. Contact your local Sure Start staff or Children's Information Service for details.

What's on offer for children with special needs?

Sure Start is keen to meet the requirements of the Disability Discrimination Act 1995 to make reasonable adjustments to activities to make them suitable for less abled children and to treat them as favourably as able children.

Opening times

Support is available year-round during office hours. Session times will vary according to the activity and site. They may also have evening and weekend sessions.

The cost of Sure Start services

Sessions are often free, but as schemes take off they may start to introduce a small charge. Check with the organizer of each activity.

How to find Sure Start

- Search www.surestart.gov.uk
- Your local Children's Information Service (CIS).
- Your local Early Years or education department.
- Posters in playgroups, primary school noticeboards, GP surgeries and baby clinics.
- Local phone directories.
- Advertisements in local newspapers.

SEE ALSO **What's best for your child?**, pages 114–116; **What's best for you?**, pages 116–118.

What is a crèche?

A crèche provides care for children under the age of eight. It needs to be registered if it is open for more than five days per year and running for more than two hours a day. You'll find different types of crèches at supermarkets and the gym, conferences and adult education classes. They are useful when you need a few hours away from your child to shop, swim or study, but you couldn't rely on them for your everyday childcare. Crèche-care can be unsettling for children, since staff may be strangers and children may not have the opportunity to get to know them before entering the room.

Type of care	Part-time
Age range	0–8 years
Hours of care	Varied
Registered and inspected	Usually
Approximate cost	£3–£5 per session per child

What a crèche does

- Provides occasional care for children under the age of eight, usually for no more than two hours at a time.

- May offer temporary facilities, such as for a time-limited, one-off activity, or permanent facilities, for instance in a health centre or gym.

- Offers play opportunities appropriate for the age and stage of the child.

- If registered, follows registration and inspection requirements laid down by the government.

Staff and qualifications

At least half the staff in registered crèches must be qualified to Level 2 or above in childcare (for details see pages 118–119). Staff under the age of 17, those who are not trained or those trained up to Level 2 are not permitted to be left on their own with children. At least one member of staff needs to be trained in first aid. Regular trainees and volunteers may be included in staffing ratios.

Minimum staff to child ratios

Age of child	Staff	Number of children
0–2 years	1	3
2 year olds	1	4
3–7 years	1	8

A minimum of two staff must be on duty at any time in registered crèches, and children of staff and volunteers must be included in ratios. The size of the group must not exceed 26 children, but there may be more than one group on the premises.

- Useful if you need to leave children for a few hours to shop, go to the gym or study.
- A great way for your child to play with other children in an informal setting.
- May accept infants: there will be a separate base area for children under two years old, with a quiet area and sleeping facilities.

POTENTIAL DISADVANTAGES

- Does not offer full-time care.
- If the crèche is only used for two hours or less it may not be registered, and so might not be up to standard.
- Surroundings and staff may be unfamiliar if the child only uses the crèche occasionally, which can be unsettling.

Who can use a crèche?

There may be restrictions on who can use the facility, for example you might need to be a member of the sports club it is set in.

What's on offer for children with special needs?

The environment, as far as reasonably possible, must be suitable for children with disabilities, and the staff should be aware that some children may have special needs and work to identify and provide for their needs.

Opening times

Hours vary to fit in with the facilities and the venue.

The cost of a crèche

May be free to members of the facility, such as a sports club; others charge £3–£5 per session per child.

How to find a crèche

- In permanent premises such as sports and shopping centres.
- Temporary and mobile provision at exhibitions, conferences or during one-off community activities.

SEE ALSO **What's best for your child?**, pages 114–116; **What's best for you?**, pages 116–118; **What makes a good childcare worker?**, pages 118–120; **What makes a good childcare facility?**, pages 121–122.

What is out-of-school care?

Kids' clubs, holiday play schemes, school breakfast and after-school clubs and summer camps all come under this catch-all title. They open before and after school and during the working day in school holidays to support parents with childcare needs. From 2006 the government is providing funding to support the development of out-of-school-hours' care. Government ministers would like primary schools to develop 'wraparound' childcare at school, so that children can be left on school premises from 8 am and picked up by 6 pm.

Type of care	Part-time
Age range	3–11 years
Hours of care	8–9 am and 3–6 pm in term-time; 9.30 am–3.30 pm during part of school holidays; hours may be 8 am–6 pm year round under the 'extended schools' initiative
Registered and inspected	Yes
Approximate cost	£7 per session or £75 per week per child

What out-of-school care does

• Looks after children before school, after school and during school holidays.

• May accept children from three years up.

• Provides play and stimulating games and activities for different age groups.

• Offers snack and drinks for children.

• May offer care in school buildings, nearby nurseries or village halls.

• Follows registration and inspection guidelines required by the government.

Staff and qualifications

At least 50 per cent of staff on duty at these clubs must hold a relevant childcare qualification at Level 2 or above (for details see pages 118–119). A minimum of two staff must be on duty at all times.

Minimum staff to child ratios

Age of child	Staff	Number of children
3–7 years	1	8

Group sizes vary, but must not exceed 26 children, although there may be more than one group on the premises.

- Convenient for working parents; you can leave children at school and not worry about picking them up within school hours.
- Affordable, quality childcare.
- Children can be cared for in a safe, familiar environment.
- Holiday clubs keep children busy and allow them to meet up with friends, mix with other adults and perhaps pursue a hobby.
- Older children enjoy skill-based holiday clubs, such as in soccer, surfing, drama or street dance.

POTENTIAL DISADVANTAGES

- May be an easy option for parents, but some children prefer a more homely environment at breakfast time and after school, such as a childminder's or friend's home.
- Some children prefer not to have to go to school during the holidays.
- 8 am to 6 pm five days a week is a long time to spend in an institution not originally set up for childcare, and is especially tiring for very young children.
- You can't control your children's diet: they may fill up on junk food.

Who can use out-of-school care?

Children between the ages of three and eleven years may attend, although in practice children don't usually attend breakfast or after-school clubs until they reach reception class, aged four or five. Holiday activities are more often pitched at junior school-aged children and above. If before- or after-school care is sited in a school, it is usually open to children from that school only. If the venue is a community hall or private day nursery, children from several schools may attend and a member of staff from the club picks children up from and delivers them to school. A holiday club based at one school or college is usually open to all children in the area, regardless of their school. Holiday clubs at venues other than schools are open to all eligible local children.

What's on offer for children with special needs?

Staff should be aware that some children may have special needs or disabilities and ensure that, where possible, they are included in appropriate activities.

Opening times

Times vary, but before-school clubs start around 8 am. After-school clubs open at the end of the school day until 5–6 pm during term-time only. Holiday clubs and summer camps are open between around 9.30 am and 3.30 pm, but do vary.

The cost of out-of-school care

Costs are approximately £7 per session or £75 per week per child at a playscheme. Holiday clubs vary according to the activity, plus the cost of a packed lunch.

How to find out-of-school care

- Newsletters and leaflets brought home from school in a child's book bag.
- Noticeboards at local primary schools, libraries and playgroups.
- Word-of-mouth recommendation.
- Your local Children's Information Service (CIS).
- Advertisements in local children's magazines.

SEE ALSO **What's best for your child?**, pages 114–116; **What's best for you?**, pages 116–118; **What makes a good childcare worker?**, pages 118–120; **What makes a good childcare facility?**, pages 121–122.

OPEN-ACCESS SCHEMES

The open-access scheme provides supervised activities in a safe environment, generally for older children (although five to seven year olds may attend). Older children are allowed to arrive and leave unaccompanied. Because the children are older, staff to child ratios are higher: minimum requirements are 1 member of staff to 13 children for five to seven year olds. Many of these schemes are short-term – a day in the park, for instance.

What is overnight care?

Some childcare facilities offer overnight care for your child, should you need it. Obviously this facility should be used sparingly, especially if your child is already in full-time day care: it's not good for children to be away from home for too many hours in a week. However, this may be your final option if you are going on a business trip, have an unexpected awkward night shift to work, or go into labour at night. You will only find formal overnight care in larger cities with a thriving business community. More often, overnight care is more informal: grandparents or other close relatives sleep in while you are out, or your child has a sleepover at a friend's home. If care takes place at your own home and children are asleep before you leave the house, make sure they know you will not be there overnight and, just as important, that they know when you will return. For more information on babysitters see pages 33–36.

Type of care	Part-time
Age range	3–16 years
Hours of care	6 pm–8 am
Registered and inspected	Possibly
Approximate cost	£7 per session or £75 per week per child, but this can vary

What an overnight carer does

- Takes charge of children for a short time only, and infrequently.

- Provides a healthy evening meal and/or snacks.

- Closely supervises children who are not in bed to make sure they are safe and happy.

- Makes time to do suitable activities with children, such as playing board games and reading stories.

- Follows the parent's bed time routine.

- Checks every half-hour to see that sleeping children are fine.

- Provides a good breakfast, if necessary.

- Ensures children are ready for school with everything they need, if necessary.

Staff and qualifications

Registered and inspected providers include staff running out-of-school clubs on summer camp, childminders and some full day-care nurseries. You might also try your regular nanny or book a professional babysitter or maternity nurse, or persuade your au pair or babysitter to sleep in.

Minimum staff to child ratios

In a childcare facility, staffing should be the same as specified in day-care regulations; check with the provider. No unauthorized person over the age of 16 must be on the premises. Staff should consult you on the overnight arrangements and you will be required to sign a contract, as for daytime care. You must inform staff of a child's medical requirements and, if medication is needed, sign a consent form.

ADVANTAGES OF USING OVERNIGHT CARE

- Helpful if you need to leave children for the night occasionally, or in a medical emergency.
- Children may enjoy spending time with adults they know well.
- Older children seem to love sleepovers at friends' homes and you save on the cost of a babysitter.

POTENTIAL DISADVANTAGES

- Overnight care in your own home is a better option, as children are able to sleep in their own beds.
- Costs can be high when using professional carers.
- The carer has to know the bed time routine of the child and be aware of comforters such as teddies or dummies.
- Your child needs to know the person who will be caring for him before you leave.
- Each child needs a suitable clean cot or bed and bedding and access to toilet and washing facilities; older children require privacy while bathing.
- You must be happy that the place is clean and hygienic, safe and secure and adequately heated.
- Food and drink must be provided to suit your children's taste and appetite.
- You must arrange for up-to-date emergency contact numbers to be on hand.

Who can use overnight care?

All who can afford it and know their children are able to cope with the separation from them overnight.

Depending on the circumstances and age of children, they may feel ill-at-ease staying overnight in an unfamiliar place. Many enjoy the occasional excitement of sleepovers and overnight visits to grandparents, but long-term would be likely to miss their own beds and parents. To ease a child's likely stress and settle him into overnight childcare it is important to let staff know about any routines or habits the child has, such as a comfort blanket, and make sure he is familiar with the place before you leave.

What's on offer for children with special needs?
Staff in facilities should be aware that some children may have special educational needs or disabilities and ensure that, where possible, they are included in activities.

Hours of care
Early evening until morning.

The cost of overnight care
Varies according to the type of a carer. Grandparents and friends usually provide services free. Contact nanny agencies and day-care nurseries with overnight facilities direct to find out their fees.

How to find overnight care
- Word-of-mouth recommendation.
- Your local Children's Information Service (CIS).
- Local telephone directories.
- Ask your child's day nursery, nanny or childminder.
- Nanny agencies.

SEE ALSO **What's best for your child?**, pages 114–116; **What's best for you?**, pages 116–118; **What makes a good childcare worker?**, pages 118–120; **What makes a good childcare facility?**, pages 121–122.

Chapter 3

Visiting a childcare provider

You might know in theory what kind of care you are looking for having read the last two chapters, but if you're considering using childcare providers outside your own home what do you ask about and look for when visiting them for the first time? In this chapter you will find accessible information on ways to judge the atmosphere, staff, and the facilities indoors and out in every type of childcare provision, from a childminder's home to a local authority nursery.

Assessing the atmosphere

When you walk into a childcare facility it is important to notice the general atmosphere. A big fancy building with all the latest equipment may look great, but it won't do your children much good if the relationship between carers and children is tense and negative. For children to thrive in a childcare facility the atmosphere needs to be positive, upbeat and happy. Use the five key areas set out below as a check list to guide you on visits to nurseries, playgroups and other formal group-care providers. You may not get the chance to consider everything on a quick visit. If you are unsure about anything it's wise to take another look before making up your mind. And remember that if you don't get the feel-good factor it is unlikely your child will either.

1 Staff/child relationships

The staff set the tone and atmosphere of a childcare facility. A key worker system should be in place where each child is allocated to a specific carer who will be responsible for ensuring that their needs are met. Key worker systems ensure continuity of care and help the child to feel secure. As in any profession, there will be some positive and well-motivated people in the job and others who do not have these qualities. When staff enjoy this job they strive to do the best for children and take pride in their work. This reflects in the atmosphere of a place, which will be light and pleasant, and you'll feel it immediately. Children who grow up in a happy atmosphere are more likely to have a high self-esteem and become happy, confident learners. They are also more anxious to please their carers, resulting in less difficult behaviour. Look for the following signs to assess how staff and children interact:

POSITIVE SIGNS FROM STAFF

- Engaging with children while they are playing.
- Talking to children at their own level, both intellectually and by squatting down to their height.
- Smiling and using encouraging gestures to the children.
- Praising and highlighting positive behaviour.
- Talking to children in a positive, encouraging way.
- Looking at ease with the children.
- Being attentive to individual children while staying aware of what is going on throughout the room.

- Showing they enjoy the company of children in their body language, for example, sitting on the floor to play rather than standing overseeing play.

- Ignoring children when they are distressed, for instance not taking children by the hand and reassuring them if they are upset on arrival.
- Belittling children when they make a mistake.
- Calling children names, such as 'silly boy'.
- Lacking interest in the children and spending time sitting talking to colleagues or other adults.
- Being short-tempered with the children.
- Shouting at and frightening children to get them to do what they want.

2 Staff/staff relationships

How staff work as a team is very important because children get caught in the crossfire of bad feelings at day care, just as they do at home with quarrelling parents. Children sense whether staff get on with each other; even if they are too young to understand what they are feeling and why, children often feel uncomfortable and maybe even a little nervous in situations of conflict. On a quick visit to a nursery it is not easy to tell if staff gel well together because they are likely to be on their best behaviour. So if you do come across a bad atmosphere between staff, have cause for concern. Ask other parents about the staff, if possible, and read the most recent inspection report, which might hint at problems.

- Engaging with each other so you can see they work as a team.
- Smiling and looking happy in each other's company.
- Talking to each other in a pleasant, positive way.
- Discussing shared social activities.

- Not looking at each other.
- Not talking to each other (though be realistic; staff who are busy with children won't always have time to chat with colleagues).

3 Staff/parent relationships

Good nurseries and playgroups have an open-door policy and are happy for parents to drop in unannounced, but, in reality, nursery schools and other formal facilities may not encourage unplanned visits: they can unsettle the children and distract staff. Play leaders may, however, be happy for you to be an extra pair of hands on outings or to help out at a set time each week, with reading for example. Some nurseries are especially welcoming if you have skills to offer – artists, drama specialists and yoga teachers, for example. It is most important to work in partnership with staff to avoid treading on toes and keep the atmosphere happy. During government inspections childcare providers have to show they are working in partnership with the parents to meet the needs of the children, which includes having mutual respect for each other.

POSITIVE SIGNS FROM STAFF

- Demonstrating real interest and pride in their work.
- Showing the same kind of values to children and parents.
- They are approachable, happy to talk to you and put you at ease.
- You get the feeling you can trust staff.
- They are professional, yet friendly and welcoming.
- They know who your child is and are keen to talk about him.
- There is a set method for exchanging information about your child, for example a diary sent home to inform you of the day's activities.
- Time is made at the end of the session to discuss the day's events.

NEGATIVE SIGNS FROM STAFF

- Looking stressed and overloaded when you approach them.
- You feel undermined and uneasy when you raise concerns.
- You are encouraged to leave quickly after a session.
- You overhear negative things about other parents.

4 Child/child relationships

If the nursery has a good general atmosphere children tend to get along and play well with each other. Of course, all children have arguments and fall out sometimes; this is their way of learning how to handle conflict. The way in which they are taught to resolve such issues reflects the attitude of the staff.

- Playing well as a group, taking turns and sharing.
- Talking to each other and treating each other with respect.
- Being busy in play.
- Looking happy together and not constantly arguing.
- Each child plays with a variety of children.

NEGATIVE SIGNS FROM CHILDREN

- Lots of fighting, pushing and arguing.
- A group or single child being nasty to one child in particular.
- Friendship groups determined by racial background.
- Either too much noise or very little.
- Not being able to play well together, even for a short length of time.

5 Children's behaviour

Children and staff obviously need to have a good relationship to get along; if they don't it shows in the atmosphere of the room.

POSITIVE SIGNS FROM CHILDREN

- Doing as they are told.
- Responding to the staff.
- Approaching the staff relaxed and happy to ask for help.
- Being attentive and concentrating on what staff say.
- Looking contented in their play and smiling.

NEGATIVE SIGNS FROM CHILDREN

- Disregarding staff instructions.
- Being loud and disruptive.
- Behaving in an unruly way or with bad behaviour.
- Seeming disinterested or unhappy.
- Not wanting to go to nursery.

SEE ALSO **Getting the best from your home carer**, pages 45–46; **Staying involved**, pages 133–136.

Checking indoor facilities

Nurseries, playgroups and childminders offer a staggeringly different range of standards in their indoor facilities for children. Large, new premises might have all the latest toys and equipment, while a smaller, older place could only contain enough facilities to meet basic needs. Most nurseries separate children of different ages into rooms containing toys and games, tables and chairs tailored to that age group, but smaller childcare providers might not have the space, staff or equipment to do this. This doesn't mean less well funded or equipped places offer worse care. Here's what to look for when checking indoor facilities:

Safety factors

If the childcare provider is registered the space will have been inspected by the local authority to make sure it is safe, secure and fit for purpose. If the provider is not registered don't consider using the care: nurseries and childminders are not allowed to operate until registered, so accept no excuses. Places that have just opened should not have to wait more than seven months for their check. Even if the space is registered, you might still like to look through the risk-assessment report and double-check on the following to lay to rest any fears:

QUESTIONS TO ASK

- **Is the room secure?** Children need to be kept in and other people kept out. There should be safety equipment such as stair gates and electrical socket covers.

- **Are children supervised at *all* times?**

- **What fire precautions are taken?** Check that fire doors are kept unobstructed and not propped open, that there are fire alarms, fire extinguishers and blankets and regular fire drills.

- **Do the premises and children look clean?** Children should be encouraged to have good personal hygiene throughout the day and toilets should be as clean late in the afternoon as they were early in the morning.

- **Are animals kept indoors?** Animals can be a health risk and may give rise to allergies. You might prefer them to be kept outside or not at all.

- **Are toys in good repair?**

- **Are walkways kept clear to prevent accidents?**

- Is a no-smoking policy strictly enforced?
- Are cots provided where babies need them, and appropriate sleeping beds for older children?

QUESTIONS FOR BABIES AND UNDER TWOS

- Is there a separate area for babies when children of all ages are together, such as in a crèche?
- Do nappy-changing facilities meet environmental health standards? (Ask to look at the risk-assessment report.)
- Is there a quiet area for sleeping?
- Are the cots used only for sleeping and not as play pens?

Toys and play equipment

Through play children learn about the world around them and develop an understanding of who they are. It is important that childcarers provide toys, games and equipment that stimulate children's senses, since this helps develop all areas of learning. When you visit a nursery or minder, check that the toys provided are appropriate for your child's age and stage of development. Also look for evidence of careful planning of toy use. Toys available should permit construction, role play and dressing up, 'small world' play, and also include puzzles and board games, books, play dough and art materials. The selection should be rotated daily, if not morning and afternoon, and all should be easily accessible. Check whether vital elements are missing – a jigsaw lacking pieces, a play cooker with no toy food, a doll with no clothes is worse than useless, leading to frustration and, eventually, disinterest, and indicates more than lack of funds.

The indoor environment

Surroundings that are welcoming, friendly, calm, happy, stimulating, colourful, structured and exciting encourage children to want to keep coming day after day. A child who wants to come to nursery will feel confident exploring the environment and this natural inquisitiveness is key to learning. When choosing childcare look around to see evidence of the following:

Inviting entrance/cloak room

Coming into nursery can be stressful for children, especially for the first time, and the cloak room can be a great place to capture their interest and help them feel welcome and part of the group. Ideally a cloak room has a peg for each child and a drawer or space for children's own belongings. Knowing where to put precious things associated with home, such as extra clothing and a favourite toy, and that they will remain safe all day makes children feel more relaxed. Pegs work best when marked clearly with the child's name and a picture they have drawn. Just as welcoming are labelled photographs of the staff and examples of current children's artwork.

Well-arranged play/care room

The best are split into different areas of play for children to explore, with enough room to move around freely. Look for all or most of the following:

- Home corner with dolls, cots, buggies, toy kitchen.
- Creative and wet play area with free access.
- Book corner/quiet area with cushions.
- Construction area for larger equipment, such as big blocks.
- Low tables and chairs for table-top toys.
- Computers are encouraged by Early Years Departments, sometimes with large, flat white boards on the wall. However, individual children should only be allowed access to computers for a few minutes a day.

Clean bathroom

Each nursery room should have an easily accessible bathroom that children can enter without leaving the enclosed, safe environment. In a nursery, toilets, basins and paper towels should be child-sized and easy to reach and warm and cold water should be provided. Reassure yourself that there is soap and toilet paper for the children to use, and do spot checks even after choosing the care centre: they can become a chore for staff to police (children love to push these items down the toilet bowl) and sometimes disappear.

Checking outdoor facilities

Outside play gives children the chance to let off steam and burn up some of their endless energy. But it does more for their development than exercise muscles and fill the lungs with fresh air: outdoor play allows children to explore the natural world and express themselves differently than they do indoors. Children who are shy inside may suddenly become uninhibited, talkative and adventurous when they emerge outdoors. Outside play should be regarded as being as important as indoor play, and good carers with the right space and equipment encourage children to move spontaneously between indoors and outdoors as much as possible. Most activities carried out indoors can just as easily be done outside, which can help with noise levels and elbow room in a less than spacious environment. Nurseries have a policy for outdoor play which you should be invited to look at, or at least welcomed to read if you ask. Childminders, playgroups or crèches may not have purpose-built facilities and space to plan elaborate outdoor play, but the best manage to make their outdoor area varied and stimulating, even if it only comprises a small concrete yard.

Imaginative play

Some childcare facilities have the financial means and room to really go to town with their outdoor play area; others may not be so lucky, but this should not stop them providing an interesting environment for children to explore. With cheap materials and a little imagination, carers might chalk a road or town for toy cars on the concrete; the children can join in and it washes away ready for some other masterpiece next time. Huge cardboard boxes can keep children happy for hours if carers use a little flair. Learning to write begins with the ability to manipulate the fingers and develop hand–eye coordination; this can just as easily be encouraged outdoors as in. Children have great fun with a pot of water and a paint brush, learning to paint marks or letters on the floor without knowing they are developing writing skills. Bikes can help children learn numbers: stick numerals on the bikes, tell a child it's his turn to ride number five and see how quickly he learns number-recognition. All areas of learning can and should be encouraged through outside play, so check that weekly plans (which should be pinned up for parents to read) include it.

Safety factors

The outdoor areas of registered childcare facilities are inspected, but keep your eyes keen for broken toys or apparatus fallen into disrepair.

- **Is wet pour (like rubber tarmac) used on climbing areas?** Bark is not recommended as animals can soil it, it is often uneven and it can hide small, harmful objects.
- **How high are the climbing frames?** Climbing frames should be no more than 2 m (6 ft) high and nuts and bolts should not protrude.
- **Where is the slide?** Slides should be built into banks where possible.
- **How secure is the outdoor play space?** The outdoor area must be enclosed by a 1.2 m (4 ft) high fence.
- **Is the sandpit covered?** Sandpits must be covered when not in use to keep them clean and prevent animals soiling them.
- **Is there a pond or pool?** Neither are permitted.
- **Are all the outdoor toys in good repair?** Broken toys must be mended or discarded.
- **Are there enough qualified staff outdoors all the time?** Staff ratios outdoors are the same as for indoors (staffing outdoor play on a cold day can be the least favoured task of some carers).
- **Does someone help children with their coats?** In cold weather coats should be done up and scarves tied safely.

The outdoor environment

Just like indoors, the outdoor play area is best divided into separate areas for different activities: to reduce accidents it makes sense to keep bikes away from sand and water or the climbing frame, for instance. Babies in a nursery require their own outdoor area and are happy playing on mats or blankets with a selection of appropriate toys. The ideal outside play area is divided into the following areas:

quiet area
Somewhere to sit, such as a bench or a rug on the grass in warm weather. Some nurseries put up a temporary gazebo for summer shade.

wheelie area
A concrete space for bikes and wheeled toys, such as wheelbarrows and carts, buggies and pull-along tyres on wheels.

climbing space
A fixed frame or moveable apparatus for climbing and balancing placed on a wet-pour surface.

growing and environmental area
Somewhere children can plant flowers, fruit and vegetables and look at insects.

construction area
A table for playing with building blocks, a mat to sit on and play with toys such as a train track, and floor space for giant building blocks. Sand and water trays might be here, too.

imaginative play area
Perhaps a Wendy house or an area to play picnics and similar games.

small apparatus area
Space for balancing beams and hoops or balls.

CHILDREN NEED THE CHANCE TO

- Climb, balance, swing, slide and jump on or over apparatus.
- Grow plants.
- Look out from, get on top of, or play inside things.
- Make music and rhyme.
- Kick, throw and aim.
- Ride, push and pull.
- Build, create, pretend.

Understanding routines and activities

Children need routines to help them feel settled and secure. If you choose childcare in your own home you can lay down the routine you would prefer your children to follow. If you decide to use childcare outside the home, your child will have to fit into an established routine. Regardless of where your child is looked after it is best if routines are structured but flexible. Even if you choose a childcare facility with very strict routines for meal times and nap times, for instance, opt for one that takes into consideration each child's needs. If your daughter needs to sleep a little longer than usual, for example, she should be allowed to eat on waking rather than being woken for food. In every place of care, time should be divided throughout the day or session between child-focused activities, where the child is free to choose what she would like to do, and adult-focused time, during which the child works under supervision on activities such as art and crafts.

Birth to three years planning

Infants and toddlers have a particular learning agenda. In England this is summed up in the Birth to Three Matters framework, upon which staff in nurseries and playgroups base their activities and care. The framework promotes development in four areas, as detailed below. If you would like to find out more about how your child's day is structured look at the Sure Start website or contact your local Children's Information Service (see Useful Contacts on page 138).

1 A strong child

For children at this stage of life, being strong is about feeling confident and learning about themselves. A key carer is vital to this development, allowing infants the support and encouragement to explore their environment, and providing lots of stimulating activities and toys.

2 A skilful communicator

To communicate effectively, babies and toddlers have to learn language and listening skills and make sense of the sounds around them. They do this by listening and responding to their surroundings, and it's especially helpful if the child's key carer plans lots of role play and conversation into the day.

3 A competent learner

To become competent learners very young children need to be creative, discovering the world through their senses. A carer encourages this by helping children explore their environment and play, first through imitating and mirroring, then by discovering for themselves through role play and interaction with others.

4 A healthy child

Being healthy as an infant means being emotionally well, staying safe and making healthy choices, that is learning to express feelings and find ways to cope with stressful situations by interacting with others and exploring the environment. A good carer ensures a child feels safe and secure and becomes attached to a key person; she also makes sure that she builds up the child's self esteem and confidence.

Early-years planning

Although each country within the United Kingdom establishes its own guidelines for early learning, all aim to provide a broad and balanced curriculum that encourages each child to reach his or her potential, regardless of ability or starting point. The ethos of early education is learning through play. Children learn best when play engages all five senses, and so a diverse and rich environment is essential for children's development. The Foundation Stage of England's National Curriculum, which prepares three to five year olds for school, is a good example of a diverse curriculum, since it divides into six distinct areas of learning. Understand these areas and the activities your child explores at day care will make more sense:

1 Physical development

Focuses on improving coordination skills and increasing control, movement and manipulation. Through play activities that encourage large and fine motor skills, children develop their physical abilities, which helps them gain confidence in themselves and enjoy being active.

2 Social and emotional development

Developing good personal, social and emotional skills is crucial for young children. It gives them the best chance to achieve in all areas of life. Childcare providers create opportunities for children to develop a positive self-image when they set up role playing in a home corner, teach about sharing toys and use group activities including story time.

3 Mathematics

Children need to be confident to learn mathematical skills. The skills encouraged at this level include counting and sorting, matching and spotting shapes and patterns. They are achieved through all sorts of activities, from songs and stories through to board games, puppets and imaginative play.

4 Communication, language and literacy

To develop speaking, listening and early writing skills children need to have confidence in themselves, be encouraged and have the opportunity to practise. Carers help promote these abilities with books and rhymes, imaginative play and by encouraging children to observe and talk to each other.

5 Knowledge and understanding of the world

Children learn to make sense of the world around them by observing, exploring, predicting, investigating and interpreting. To do this they need their carers to provide a variety of materials and tools, from seeds and plant pots to tape measures and growth charts.

6 Creative development

The ability to be creative is essential if children are to develop in all areas of learning. Creativity through dance, music, art, craft activities and imaginative play helps children connect together and make sense of different types of knowledge and understanding. It should be encouraged by all good childcarers.

Understanding registration and inspection

England, Scotland, Wales and Northern Ireland have different registration and inspection bodies for early-years care. They do, however, all follow similar guidelines that put the interests of the child first and ensure children are cared for in a safe, happy, stimulating environment that provides for all their developmental needs. Each registered childcare provider will have a report from the relevant inspection agency. You should ask to see this report and read it before signing up your child for care with that provider. You might like to check out nursery, playgroup and nursery school reports online via each inspection body's website (see Useful Contacts on pages 138).

England's guidelines on early-years standards

Ofsted (Office for Standards in Education) is responsible for the registration and inspection of voluntary, independent and local authority early-years providers. All childminders and day-care providers must be registered with Ofsted, which evaluates the standards of care and education given to ensure that they meet national standards for children under eight. Ofsted inspectors also assess the progress children make toward early learning goals, including the Birth to Three Matters guidelines and the Foundation Stage curriculum for three to five year olds detailed on pages 104–106. Ofsted inspects a new childcare provider within seven months of opening and then yearly.

Scotland's guidelines on early-years standards (Care Commission)

SCRC (Scottish Commission for the Regulation of Care) is responsible for the registration and inspection of voluntary, independent and local authority early-years providers. It evaluates the care of all childminders and day-care providers to ensure it meets the standards set by the National Care Standards for Early Education in Childcare up to 16 years. Inspectors also assess children's progress toward the Birth to Three Matters guidelines commissioned by the Scottish Executive and the Scottish Curriculum framework for three to five year olds. Carers are inspected every year to ensure that standards are continually met.

Wales' guidelines on early-years standards

CSIW (Care Standards Inspectorate for Wales) is responsible for the registration and inspection of early-years providers in Wales to ensure they comply with the Care Standards Act 2000 and the Children Act 1989. Inspection and registration follows national minimum standards set by the Welsh Assembly for childminders and day-care providers. Estyn, Her Majesty's Inspectorate for Education and Training in Wales, inspects the funded part-time education provisions for 3- and 4-year-olds in non-maintained nursery settings. The progress of children is assessed against the Desirable Outcomes for Children's Learning before Compulsory School Age published by the Qualifications, Curriculum and Assessment Authority for Wales (ACCAC). From September 2008 there will be new guidelines for the Foundation Phase for children's learning from 3–7 years.

Northern Ireland's guidelines on early-years standards

Pre-school guidelines are currently under review; contact your local authority for the latest information.

Questions to ask

If you are interested in a nursery or other childcare facility the first thing to do is ask the manager for a prospectus or information pack or visit the website if there is one. This may cut down on the number of questions you need to ask when visiting the premises and give you greater insight into how the care works. When you arrange to visit, do so while it is in full session. A good childcarer will understand that you have lots of questions and be happy to answer them. She should offer to show you around the whole facility and into each room, including the kitchen and bathrooms; nowhere should be out of bounds. First impressions are very important; you may know as soon as you walk through the door whether the place and people feel right.

Before you go

Visiting a nursery or other care provider can be overwhelming; it's often best to sit down the day before and write out the questions you would like answered. Ask your partner or a close friend who is also a parent to brainstorm questions with you. Note down the answers as you walk around the premises so you can ponder them later at home. Here are some questions you may like to ask:

QUESTIONS ON DAY-TO-DAY CARE

- How many children do you care for?
- Which room would my child be in?
- Where would my child have a sleep?
- How do you get them to go to sleep?
- What will my child be doing all day/for the session?
- What sort of routine is there?
- Do the children play outdoors every day?
- Can I see the weekly activity plan?
- What sort of food and drink do you provide?
- Can you cater for special dietary needs?
- How do you deal with picky eaters?
- Do children have a snack in the morning and afternoon? If so can they bring their own? Is anything not allowed?
- Do children have access to drinking water throughout the day?

- How do you settle children in?
- How do you cater for children with special needs?
- Will my child have a key worker?
- How can I make sure my child is getting on well?
- Am I expected to help out?
- Can I see the current registration certificate and the latest inspection report?

QUESTIONS ON COSTS

- How much are the fees?
- When and how would I pay the fees?
- Is there a registration fee?
- What about the cost of meals?
- Do I have to pay if my child is absent with sickness or on holiday?
- Do you offer free sessions for three and four year olds?
- Are you well funded for the long-term?

QUESTIONS ON STAFFING

- What sort of qualifications and experience do staff have?
- Do you have a high staff turnover?
- How long have you worked with children?
- How long have you worked here?
- What staff ratios do you use?
- Do you use students?
- Who would be my child's main carer/s?
- How do you handle children's misbehaviour?

QUESTIONS ON HOURS

- What hours are you open?
- When do you close during the year?
- Do you offer care for older siblings during school holidays?

Chapter 4

Making the right choice

Now you have all the options in front of you, have made some visits and asked all the right questions, it's time to make your childcare choice. In this chapter a step-by-step guide steers you through the process while summaries and useful check lists remind you of what makes a good care worker and how to spot a caring place for your child to spend time. At the end of the day, no matter which childcare option you are weighing up, trust your instincts: you are the one who knows your child's personality, abilities and needs best of all.

Step-by-step guide to making a choice

If you still feel confused and don't know where to start, try these easy-to-follow steps to help you to choose the type of care that will best suit you and your child.

1 Start looking early

No matter which kind of care you decide on, finding the right person or place can take some time. To avoid the disappointment of finding the right place or nanny is fully booked, it is best to start looking early. Some carers and nurseries have long waiting lists and you may need to have your name down many months in advance. Second-time parents often put down a sibling's name just after birth to ensure the right care. It can take many weeks to find a nanny, interview her and then make arrangements for her to start work. Some nursery schools have a set intake date, so to make sure your child can be involved from the beginning of term, you may have to wait a few months.

2 Gather information

To make a well-informed decision about what type of childcare is best for you and your child, it's helpful to collect information about the options from a variety of sources.

HOW TO DO IT

- Read books.
- Talk to local parents, the source of the most realistic information, and ask them for recommendations.
- See what's available in your area by looking in local telephone directories.
- Contact your local Children's Information Service (CIS) or the Early Years Department of your education authority for lists of local carers and nurseries.
- Contact agencies for lists of nannies and other home-based care providers.
- Telephone nurseries, playgroups, minders and other childcarers to ask for information and a prospectus or leaflets.
- Contact your local Early Years Department for information on how care providers in your area are regulated (see pages 106–107).

3 Make your choice

Collate all the information you have collected and think about the hours of childcare you need. Remember to add in commuting times and settling-in time on arrival if you are using carers outside your home. You might want to rethink your own routines and those of your partner. If you are returning to work after having your first child it is unlikely that your day will run exactly as it did before, so try to keep your options open. Next do a financial check, writing down all your monthly incomings and outgoings: can you afford the type of childcare you have highlighted as the best? If you have a partner you might want to consider one of you reducing your hours, job-sharing or taking a sabbatical while children need full-time care (before they start school full-time).

HOW TO DO IT

- Assess your needs using the charts on pages 13–15, ticking the columns that work for you.

- Reassess your thoughts by considering what your child needs using the same charts. Have you ticked the same columns?

- Read the pages outlining the type of care that correlate with the columns you have ticked. When you have earmarked a short list of types of care that would work for you, try to match these up with the leaflets and information you have collected locally. You may not get an exact match; there may not be the type of care you would prefer near your home, so try to remain open to alternatives.

- Look again at your finances and what sort of financial assistance you may be entitled to (see pages 16–17). Can you afford the care you would like or will you have to compromise?

4 Visit and interview

Once you have a shortlist of options, make arrangements to visit providers outside the home, such as nurseries and childminders, or, if you think you would like childcare at home, arrange to talk to potential carers and arrange an interview, possibly in your home. You might have to approach carers via agencies or your local Children's Information Service.

HOW TO CHECK A HOME CHILDCARE PROVIDER

- Make telephone contact first to see how you feel about each carer.

- Read candidates CVs and make lists of questions to ask.

- Arrange to meet several carers for an interview (see pages 42–45).

- Consider the qualities of a good childcare worker and whether this person seems to meet them (see pages 40–42 and 118–120).
- Obtain at least two references from your preferred carer; call previous employers if you have outstanding queries.
- Introduce your child to the carer to see how they interact.
- Trust your instinct.
- When you are ready to commit, sign a contract, but don't feel pressurized into making a decision by an agency (see pages 124–128).

HOW TO CHECK AN OUTSIDE CHILDCARE PROVIDER

- Check the outdoor facilities (see pages 101–103).
- Check the indoor facilities (see pages 98–100).
- Assess the atmosphere of the place (see pages 94–97).
- Look at the routines and activities (see pages 104–106).
- Have a list of questions ready to ask (see pages 108–109).
- Consider the qualities of a good childcare worker and whether these workers seem to meet them (see pages 118–120).
- Trust your instinct.
- When you are ready to commit, sign a contract, but don't feel pressurized into making a decision on the spot (see pages 124–128).

What's best for your child?

When you are considering childcare options, the thought underlying every decision you make should be 'What is best for my child?' In order to flourish, children need to spend their days in a safe, stimulating environment surrounded by adults who care for them and provide for all their needs to promote every area of development. When thinking about the best practical option for your child it pays to reflect on the child's personality and age as well as how many hours' care are needed. Here is more information about these three key factors:

1 Your child's personality
Considering your child's personality style helps you choose a style of childcare into which she will fit and be happy. Here are some common personality types:

The outgoing child

Some children like to be the centre of attention and are eager to join in with new activities. They enjoy being kept busy and enjoying the company of other children their age. But this much energy also needs channelling into appropriate activities to make sure children don't become over-boisterous. A nanny may be able to keep outgoing children busy with a full schedule and arranging for friends to come over, but outgoing children might be happiest in a large, boisterous nursery with lots of other children to play with and well structured, adult-led activities. A smaller establishment with few children their own age probably won't suit as well.

The shy, quiet child

Children who might be shy until they get to know people (when they come out of their shell) may not particularly like lots of noise, and large groups of children can make them feel nervous and inhibited. They need lots of reassurance and time to adjust, and may prefer a more homely environment, such as a childminder's house or a nanny at home. Quiet children may take a while to make new friends and adjust to childcare, so try to choose one type of care and stick with it rather than using more than one.

The easy-going child

Between the two previous personality types, easy-going children are equally happy in large, loud groups of children and in a quieter setting. They are pretty adaptable to change and make friends easily. An easy-going child will enjoy a variety of settings and might be able to shift between them, for instance spending time with a childminder and attending a playgroup.

2 The child's age

The age of your child limits the type of care available, since children may not join certain playgroups or nursery classes until they reach a set age. Different age groups need varying things from childcare and you may like to consider the following:

The birth to two year old

Babies and toddlers require a stable environment and a familiar carer to bond with, and might be best at home with a nanny or in a small group of children with a childminder. In a day-care nursery, assess the staff turnover and setting carefully to make sure children this young have the space and encouragement to explore while learning to walk and talk. This age group is generally kept together in a nursery, although some may be moved to an older peer group at 18 months, if the child seems ready and places are available.

The two to three year old

Children of this age are learning many new skills, such as talking, socializing, toilet training, and fine and large motor development. As they enjoy playing alongside other children and role playing, now might be the time to explore care in group settings, such as a playgroup or nursery, if only for a few hours a week. Here they can experiment with dressing up and making friends in the home corner as they learn about themselves.

The three to five year old

At this stage, children are developing abilities that prepare them for school, the older ones becoming familiar with numbers and letters and developing early writing skills. At the same time they are learning social skills and starting to play together rather than side by side, so being able to mix with peers is very important. Groups of the same age children are a distinct advantage now. This age group is developing a greater concentration span and may enjoy the kind of adult-focused activities you find at a nursery school.

3 The number of hours' care

Considering how many hours your child needs to be looked after is a great help in whittling down your childcare options. If, for example, you need childcare for 40 hours every week you need to look for either a full-time daycare provider, such as a nursery outside the home or a nanny indoors, or, more complex to arrange, a mixture of two facilities, such as a playgroup and a childminder. The least complicated option is not always the best.

What's best for you?

There is nothing more important as a parent than knowing your child is happy throughout the day, no matter what he is doing. To turn the tables, the very best thing you can do for your child is also to be happy in what you are doing. If you are miserable with your childcare arrangements for any reason, your child is likely to suffer by picking up on your mood. Here are some questions to help you double-check that this option is the best option in the real world; you may find the answers reassuring.

Practical questions to ask yourself

FINANCIAL ISSUES

- Can you afford the fees and any hidden extras that may arise, such as trips and equipment?
- Can you claim any financial assistance for the childcare place (see pages 16–17)?

HOURS AND WORK

- Does the care provider offer long-enough hours to cover your work and travel commitments?
- Can you realistically manage the journey to this facility day in, day out?
- If there is a gap between your childcare and work finish times can someone pick up your child, such as a childminder?
- Do you feel comfortable sending your child to the facility for the amount of hours he needs to spend there?
- If you work long hours will you have enough time left in the day to see your child?
- How many hours a day do you want/need to work? How about your partner?
- If you don't need to work full-time would you be happier working fewer hours a week?
- Do you think you can balance the amount of hours you have to work with being a parent and looking after a household?
- If not, how many hours' work do you need to do to meet the needs of your finances, your child and yourself?

EMOTIONAL ISSUES

- How do you feel about your child forming an intensely close relationship with a carer?
- If you are still breast-feeding, how will you cope at your baby's feed times emotionally as well as practically?
- How will you feel if you have to give up nursing?
- Will you regret missing milestones such as the first step or word?
- Do you have a support system at home, such as a partner to help out with housework and extended family to cover when your child is ill?

Positive aspects of choosing the right childcare

- Going to work usually means you are better off financially.
- You will be able to enjoy the benefits of pursuing a career.
- You may be able to do some further study or train in new skills.

BENEFITS FOR YOU

- Enjoying a break from child and home may mean you are happier when you are with each other.
- You may have a little more time to yourself, especially if your child goes out to a nursery and you do not work.
- Most parents meet other parents via childcare who become good friends and provide support.
- You might be able to volunteer at a playgroup or nursery, which not only boosts your skills and self-esteem (for some parents it opens up a new career path), it gets you out of the house mixing with new people.

BENEFITS FOR YOUR CHILD

- Gaining skills that will help at school; good early-years education gives children a head start.
- Making close friends who can come home to play; they may move on to school with friends they have made.

What makes a good childcare worker?

Having a qualification in childcare is not the only quality of a good childcare worker: indeed, some childcare workers, such as childminders and nannies, are not qualified but do an excellent job. And you certainly don't need a childcare qualification to be a good parent. But, as a general rule, you are more likely to have high quality childcare if carers are well educated, especially if they have a childcare qualification. A training in childcare shows a commitment to and interest in working with children. Registered childcare providers also need to have at least 50 per cent of their staff trained in childcare. The qualifications they might have are set out below, along with a summary of other qualities to look for in someone who works with children.

Childcare qualifications

A vast array of childcare qualifications are offered in England and Northern Ireland. Recognized qualifications are awarded by the Council for Awards in Children's Care and Education (CACHE), associated institutions that are members of the Association of Nursery Training Colleges, and the Business and Technology Education Council (BTEC). In Scotland, the Scottish Child Care and Education Board (SNNB) is responsible for awarding childcare qualifications, in Wales it is the Qualifications, Curriculum and Assessment Authority for Wales (ACCAC). Changes in qualifications occur regularly; for the latest information contact the Qualifications and Curriculum Authority (QCA) or the bodies detailed above (see Useful Contacts on pages 138–139).

CACHE QUALIFICATIONS

- **CACHE Level 2 (CCE) in Childcare and Education** One year full-time foundation course.
- **CACHE Level 3 (DCE) in Childcare and Education** (previously the NNEB certificate) Two year full-time course equivalent to two A levels.

BTEC QUALIFICATIONS

- **BTEC National Certificate in Childhood Studies** Part-time course equivalent to two A levels or NVQ Level 3 (see below).
- **BTEC Higher National Diploma (HND) Childhood Studies/Nursery Nursing** Full-time course equivalent to first year of a degree.
- **BTEC National Diploma in Childhood Studies** Two year full-time course equivalent to first two years of a degree.
- **DPP Diploma in Play Group Practice** One year course covering all areas of development, with an emphasis on learning through play.

NVQ QUALIFICATIONS

- **NVQ Level 3 in Childcare and Education** Equivalent to CACHE Level 3 qualification and NNEB certificate (see above).
- **NVQ Level 4 in Childcare and Education** More advanced and academically challenging, taking students up to management level.

Qualities to look for in a carer

The qualities of the ideal childcare worker are listed below and there are plenty of excellent staff who strive to meet these standards. As parents we need workers to share these qualities because how they interact with children not only governs the way in which children respond to them, but has a huge impact on child development. And if carer and parent share the qualities listed, children develop independence and self-control, become active and outgoing, sociable and spontaneous. They also grow up to be healthy, positive, self-confident, happy learners who reach their full potential.

IDEAL CHILDCARER QUALITIES

- Attentive and responsive to children's needs.
- Enjoys the company of children.
- Sets boundaries, rules and consequences for misbehaviour.
- Uses rewards and praise for good behaviour.
- Does not use harsh punishments.
- Motivates children to live up to expectations.
- Talks respectfully to parents and children.
- Communicates well with parents and children.
- Understands child development.
- Fulfils children's nutritional requirements.
- Creates a stimulating, calm, happy environment.
- Provides structure and routine throughout the day to channel children's energy appropriately.
- Has a rapport with the children.
- Approachable.
- Endlessly patient.
- Good sense of humour.
- Caring and compassionate in nature.
- Confident with children and their parents.
- Up-to-date first-aid skills.
- Aware of health and safety issues.

What makes a good childcare facility?

Whichever type of childcare provision you choose, it will have similar attributes if it's of the best quality; these characteristics are listed below. Even if children are staying at home with a nanny you can work with her to ensure they benefit from most of the same features. You can even request registration to make nanny care more like that of a nursery, now nannies can be registered under the Childcare Approval Scheme (see pages 51–52). When children are cared for in the right kind of environment they feel secure and confident enough to use their natural inquisitiveness to explore the world around them, which develops all areas of learning. Here's what to look for or strive to create; add to the lists your own priorities, too.

How to spot good staff
- A great reputation.
- They share the qualities of a good childcare worker (see pages 118–120).
- Appropriate staff ratios (see each type of care setting, pages 48–91).
- Low staff turnover.
- A happy atmosphere between staff and children (see pages 94–97).
- Good salaries and benefits.

How to spot thriving children
- They look happy and well cared for.
- Most of them are clean and tidy.
- Children play well together.
- All ages are well supervised.
- They are engaged in appropriate activities.
- Most of the children are behaving appropriately most of the time.

How to spot a good environment
- It is secure.
- The entrance is welcoming and the rest of the space inviting.
- There is an emphasis on healthy eating.

- Special dietary requirements are catered for.
- Children have access to drinking water when they want it.
- Activities are stimulating, structured and creative.
- The atmosphere seems nurturing and calm.
- There is plenty of space indoors and out and it is well used.
- Everything is clean and safety-checked.
- Age-appropriate toys and activities are arranged indoors and out.
- There is opportunity to play outside.
- Well-planned schedules devote time for adult- and child-focused activities.
- Children are learning about different cultures.
- Equipment is of a high standard, ample in variety and child-sized, where appropriate.
- If younger children are cared for there are facilities for baby changing and potty training.
- Beds and cots are provided for children who need to sleep.
- Written policies and procedures are easily accessible to parents.
- Staff and routines are flexible.
- Learning through play is the basis of the day.
- Ground rules are clearly established and both the children and parents know them.
- You are able to inspect the current registration certificate and latest inspection report.
- There is an open-door policy.
- Plenty of current children's drawings and paintings are on display.

Chapter 5

Having made your choice

Congratulations! You have chosen who will look after your child and where your child will spend time away from you. Now down to the practicalities. This chapter contains information on drawing up contracts for workers in your home and a sample contract you might be asked to sign at a nursery or playgroup. There is also information on settling your child in and monitoring his or her progress, as well as signs to watch for that might indicate that your child is not thriving – and what to do to remedy such problems.

Sample contracts

To prevent ambiguity and any misunderstanding of what is required from you and your childcarer, it is important to have a contract of employment, whether you are taking your child out each day to a nursery or using a formal worker, such as a nanny, in your own home. (Informal childcarers such as babysitters and au pairs do not need a contract unless you feel it appropriate.) In a nursery or other formal care setting the contract may be known as a conditions of admission document and should set out the policies and procedures of the establishment on matters such as discipline and equal opportunities. By law, childminders need to have a written contract with the parents or guardian of every child they look after. This aims to clear up any ambiguities about tasks and responsibilities and, ideally, is reviewed by both parties every six to twelve months. Contracts are legally binding and any alterations must be agreed and signed by both parties. If drawing up your own contract you might like to base the details on the following templates, but feel free to add more details to suit your circumstances. Alternatively, the Early Years Department of your local authority might be able to provide a pre-printed contract.

Sample contract for a childcarer in your home

- Date of issue.
- Employer's name, address and telephone number.
- Employee's name, address and telephone number.
- Job title.
- Place of work.
- Name of child.
- Birth date of child.
- Date employment starts.

duties (make specific to your family)

- To be in sole charge of the children while on duty.
- To provide the children with nutritionally balanced meals.
- To provide stimulating activities for the children each day, indoors and out.
- To take older children to and from school.

- To wash the children's laundry.
- To read to the children, or hear them read, each day for 15 minutes at bed time.
- To bathe children each day before bed.

special needs requirements

authority to administer medication/act *in loco parentis* for emergency medical treatment/hospital care

hours of work
To include days off per week and when they may be taken, plus babysitting hours per week, if applicable.

salary details
- Amount of salary per annum (state that the employee will pay national insurance and tax).
- Date of salary payment and means of payment.
- Overtime payment/time off in lieu.
- Annual salary review date.

extra costs
- Including for children's meals, drinks, snacks, nappies, toiletries, transport, outings, playgroup and activity fees and other costs.

sick pay
The employee will be entitled to full sick pay starting three weeks after commencement of employment and full pay will be paid for … weeks, by which time the employee will be entitled to the government's statutory sick pay.

holiday entitlement
- Holiday entitlement per year is … starting on the 1st day of employment.
- The employee can/cannot carry forward holiday to the following year.
- The employee is entitled to take bank holidays off or take time off in lieu.

maternity entitlement
- The carer is entitled to Statutory Maternity Pay (SMP).

other entitlement

- The employee is entitled to all meals; this includes/does not include on days off.
- The employee is entitled to free accommodation with/without a private bathroom.
- The employee may/may not use the family car when not on duty.
- The employee will receive … per mile petrol allowance for use of her own car while on duty.

pension

The employer does/does not provide a pension scheme.

retainer to secure place

notice period

The employee/employer may terminate employment by giving … weeks' notice.

details of trial period

A four-week trial period is recommended.

confidentiality

- Employees are to keep the affairs and business of the household confidential at all times.

details of disciplinary procedures

sackable offences

- Failure to comply with the duties set out in the contract.
- Bad timekeeping or attendance.
- Breach of confidentiality.
- Job incompetence.
- Being a disruptive influence on the household.
- Bad conduct during or out of working hours.

employee's signature and employer's signature

Sample contract for a childminder

- Date of issue.
- Childminder's name, address and telephone number.
- Parent's name, address and telephone number.
- Child's name.
- Birth date of child.
- Starting date.

availability
Including evenings, weekends and overnight, if applicable.

who is allowed to pick up child
Include details of password, if applicable.

special needs requirements

authority to administer medication/act *in loco parentis* for emergency medical treatment/hospital care

fees
Including daily/weekly rate, over-hours rate, and discounted rate for siblings, if applicable. Also, when and how fees are to be paid.

extra costs
Including for meals, drinks, snacks, nappies, toiletries, transport, outings, playgroup and activity fees and other costs.

holiday and sickness fees
- What is or isn't paid during the child's or childminder's holidays or sickness.
- Details of the childminder's back up (if applicable) during illness/holidays.

deposit or retainer to secure place

period of notice to be given on either side; details of trial period
A four-week trial period is recommended.

childminder's signature and parent's signature

Sample contract for full day care, sessional care and out-of-school care

- Date of issue.
- Nursery's name, address and telephone number.
- Name of manager.
- Parent's name, address and telephone number.
- Name of child.
- Birth date of child.
- Starting date.
- Dates and times of attendance.

fees
Including hourly/sessional/daily or weekly fees, late pick-up fees and discounted rate for siblings, if applicable. Also when and how fees are to be paid.

extra costs
Including for meals, drinks, snacks, nappies, toiletries, transport and outings.

holiday and sickness fees
Whether full or no fees are paid during the child's holidays or sickness.

deposit or retainer to secure place

details of trial period

additional information
Including who is allowed to pick up the child, allergies, dietary requirements, special needs, ethnicity and religion. Permission for the child to be photographed or videoed, go on outings, travel in a vehicle or take part in water-based activities.

manager/supervisor's signature and parent's signature

Settling your child in

Easing your child out of your care and into someone else's can be very stressful and emotional for parents and child alike. Happily, there are many things you can do to help make the transition as smooth as possible. The key to settling her in as smoothly as possible is to be prepared and to stay positive. Talk to the carer about your concerns (every parent has some); she, too wants your child to settle as soon as possible and should be able to offer advice and reassurance.

Be prepared

Being well prepared for your child's first day away from you starts with getting all your children into a routine of going to bed and getting up early for some time before the big day. Children who are rushed out of the house in the morning and dropped off in a hurry often get anxious and irritable because they don't have enough time to adjust. So do children whose parents dash out of the house the second the nanny comes through the door. Children are usually much more cooperative if they are up and ready to go in good time, ideally with a short time at home to play before they go out or a carer arrives. Here are some more suggestions for being well prepared:

WHAT TO DO

- Get children used to spending time without you by having a friend or relative occasionally take care of them during the day.
- Make sure children have spent time mixing with other children to develop their social skills.
- Try to find some playmates who already attend the nursery so your child can make friends before starting (if old enough).
- Talk to your child, even if still a baby, explaining where she is going, who she will meet, what she will do and why she needs a carer.
- Read books about going to nursery to make the idea seem more real.
- Reassure your child that she will be fine.
- Drive or walk past the venue so you can talk about it together.
- Take your child for a few short visits to look around and meet the staff before the start date (may be easier with a flexible childminder than a nursery school that may like to tie in new intake visits to one open day).

- Make sure your child is as independent as possible in preparation for attending a nursery. Four year olds, for instance, are more confident and find life at nursery less stressful if they can do up their own coat and shoes.

- Before a home carer, such as a nanny, starts make sure she knows the layout of the house and toy cupboards, that she knows your child's favourite games and foods, and knows exactly what she's supposed to do all day.

- Make sure you have public liability insurance, if required, for your home carer so you can relax about accidents.

Stay positive

It is so important to be positive to children about starting with a new carer. Even if you feel miserable about it, try not to let it show. If you are negative and say things like, 'You have to go to nursery or the police will take mummy away,' while crying in the entrance clutching your child (I have seen it done), you cause the child great stress. Here are alternative coping strategies:

WHAT TO DO

- Children need to know you feel happy with the idea of them being away from you so they don't have to worry about your feelings, so be sure to keep making this point in conversation.

- If your child is having problems separating from you, give him something familiar from home, such as a blanket or teddy, for comfort. But check with the nursery or playgroup before sending a toy with an older child.

- Remember that some children need longer to settle into new surroundings and get used to you coming and going.

- Consider the age and personality of your child. Some children walk into day care full of confidence and anticipation and eager to make new friends only to lose confidence a few weeks down the line; some hide behind their parent's legs crying and wanting to go home; others need a little encouragement and a reassuring hand to hold as parents leave.

- Keep being positive even if your child cries every morning for a few weeks (but ask for reassurance from staff that there are no real problems).

The first day

If you've followed the advice above you should be well prepared and positive when the big day comes. Make sure you have taken care of all the time-consuming 'official' matters beforehand so you can focus fully on the leaving bit. This includes having signed the contract or admission form, left emergency contact numbers and details of allergies, medical conditions and special dietary needs, and briefed carers about your child's routines, sleep and feeding patterns. It is enormously helpful to children if you have a goodbye routine planned to help them understand what's going on and what to expect next. Ideally you should start using it before they start childcare so it feels perfectly normal. Adapt the routine below to suit the age of your child:

The goodbye routine

1 Arrive early, allowing yourself time before you have to leave to settle your child in by hanging up his coat and putting his belongings away.

2 Say hello to the staff and, if the child can, encourage him to do the same. You need acknowledgement that staff know your child is in their care and has arrived.

3 Try to encourage your child to start an activity. Most nurseries have toys out when children arrive to entice them to join in and play. If there is a different routine, such as sitting together while the register is taken, be prepared to follow it.

4 Tell your child you are going to leave now and say goodbye. When you have decided to leave do so straight away. Don't accidentally reward a child's behaviour by staying if he cries. It might be the hardest thing in the world to leave your child crying, but it is far harder for him to deal with if he doesn't know the boundaries and you only prolong the agony. Your child will wonder where you are going, so tell him you are going to work if that is true or that you are doing something boring, like ironing, so he doesn't feel he is missing out on anything. Pass a crying child to a member of staff as soon as you can; if staff are busy with someone else, wait a short time if you can, until they become free.

5 Never be tempted to sneak out while your child is not looking; this exacerbates a tense situation and makes your child distrust you. Your child may become more clingy and nervous, wondering when you are going to leave next time.

6 If you have left your child crying and want to know how he is doing, ring the nursery after half an hour. Most children settle within a minute or two and it is a shame to worry all morning when your child is having fun after all. Staff should call you if your child continues to be upset throughout the day.

The first weeks

The next few weeks can be an anxious time as you settle into the new routine. It is important to stick to your routines and to ensure that your child is getting plenty of rest and good food to keep energy levels high. Spend time with your child every day after childcare to prevent misbehaviour to grab your attention. Here are a few more suggestions to get you through the first few weeks:

HOW TO COPE

- Talk to your child if you can and the carer to see how both are getting on and what they have enjoyed and not enjoyed.

- Be prepared for your child to be more enthusiastic on some days than others.

- Speak to staff if there is something important they should know, for example that your child had a disturbed night or would not eat breakfast; this helps build a relationship with carers.

- Talk to other parents for support and to share ideas; why not suggest a social evening for parents of new children?

- Become involved with the parent committee or association if you would like to feel part of the group.

- Don't forget to take care of yourself: unwind and relax when you can to recoup the energy reserves needed to cope with the stresses of family life.

THE CHILD'S POINT OF VIEW

Being praised for good behaviour encourages children when they are settling into a new routine without you. A child who is left crying in the morning but settles later gains in self-confidence when he hears you saying, 'Your nanny said you played really nicely this morning; shall we go to the park because you have been so good?'

Staying involved

Now you've found a carer and settled your child in, don't think this is the end. The secret to continuing happy care is for you to stay involved and to develop, and maintain, a good relationship with your child's carer.

The essentials

Do these few things and you can't fail to promote good working relations, keep your child's progress and happiness at the top of your agenda, and stop bad situations from developing in the early stages:

- Talk to your child's carer each day, for example about potty training or behaviour issues.

- Get involved with the facility where possible: offer to help out with reading, art or outdoor games; be an extra pair of hands on trips out; get stuck into fundraising; attend AGMs and parent-teacher meetings.

- Assess and review your child's changing needs every now and then – every six months perhaps – looking at whether this new age stage or your home or work routine requires changes in childcare.

The importance of communication

Without good – and reciprocal – communication, you will not be able to build a good relationship with your child's carer. Registered childcare providers are required to ensure they work in partnership with parents, but you'll have to do the running with non-registered carers, such as au pairs and family members.

HOW TO DO IT

- Make an opportunity at the beginning and end of the day to exchange essential information, such as sleep and eating patterns and health issues.

- Look at your children's work: drawings, paintings and craft work should be displayed for parents to see.

- Learn about the key worker system, if there is one: your child is allocated a worker who takes responsibility for his welfare; you then always know who to talk to about your child.

- Ask for regular, longer meetings to discuss progress and concerns.

- Make sure you're aware of policies and procedures and the discussions of daily routines registered facilities have to minute.

- Scan noticeboards for details of what children are doing each day; the timetable should be displayed prominently, alongside requests for your old yogurt pots and cardboard boxes for craft activities.

- Give full, up-to-date contact details to carers and notify them of any changes immediately; you should expect to be notified in turn of changes in staff or premises.

- When your role is explained to you – for example having to work on a playgroup rota or attend a certain number of meetings – make sure you listen, take notes, if necessary, and fulfil your obligations.

- Parents views and concerns are taken seriously by good carers, and registered staff must maintain privacy and confidentiality at all times, so don't be afraid to speak out and follow up concerns.

- You have right of access to all records written about your child; don't forget to pick them up when your child moves on.

- If you have a child with special needs ensure a nursery contacts all the relevant refereeing agencies.

When problems occur

Talk to your child's carer as soon as any problems occur, no matter how small, and try to work toward a solution together. The behaviour of children can sometimes change for the worse when they are facing stress of some kind, and as moving away from your sole care is inevitably stressful for a child, you might anticipate common problems:

SIGNS TO WATCH FOR

- Reversion to infant ways, such as wanting a dummy or talking in a baby voice.
- Clinginess.
- Tears and over-wrought emotions.
- Fighting with siblings.
- Biting other children.
- Disobedience.
- Soiling or wetting themselves when they have been dry for some time.

How to manage difficult behaviour

While it is obviously a concern if your child starts to display difficult, unruly behaviour, it is important to stay firm but fair. Children test boundaries and if they cannot find any become anxious, which can make bad behaviour worse. Of course, you should address any concerns with the care provider and keep a check for more worrying signs of abuse (see pages 136–137), but just managing children's behaviour appropriately helps them feel secure and loved, which is what they need when they start day care and may, in time, be enough to solve the problem. Above all they need extra love and attention right now. To prevent escalating behaviour problems, it helps to understand common types of childhood behaviour:

1 Age-related behaviour

This is the difficult behaviour you expect from a child because she is at a certain age. For instance, toddlers learning to feed themselves are bound to make a mess, drop the spoon and spill the drink. Age-related behaviour is normal and to be expected, and the best way to manage problems is to encourage children to learn the skill that they are trying to master. Try breaking it down into manageable chunks and mastering one stage before progressing to the next. You could help a child who is learning to feed herself by showing how to pick finger foods up first to gain fine motor skills; the next stage is learning to hold a spoon, then, with your hand as guidance, scooping up food with it. Follow children's developmental stages, teaching them at their own pace and the problem will resolve itself.

2 Childish behaviour

All parents sometimes think children do irritating things, including tantrums, screaming and shouting for what they want, just to annoy us. The best way to manage tantrums is to ignore them: respond and you may escalate and prolong the bad behaviour. Do the same when they scream, shout and kick you to get your attention, adding that you will talk to them when they speak nicely to you.

3 Disobedient behaviour

When a child is not doing as you ask, her behaviour becomes unacceptable and needs to be nipped in the bud to stop it from escalating. Try the following coping strategies and stick to them: when a child knows what to expect it's easier on you both in the long run.

Ask for the behaviour you want Say, 'Keep the toys on the table', instead of, 'Stop throwing the toys'. Children hear 'Toys on the table' or 'Throwing the toys' and act likewise. It's simple but very effective.

Follow through with consequences If children don't do as you ask, a logical action is to make them stop what they are doing, for example take away the toys they are playing with for five minutes. If they continue once you have given the toys back, ask them again with the same consequence. If they repeat the behaviour, increase the consequence, perhaps some quiet time out from playing. You could sit them on the sofa for a minute for each year of their age. If they still misbehave progress to time out in a quiet, safe, well-lit room. Start counting the time when they are quiet (or quietening down), letting them out when they have calmed down. This might sound cruel but it is a very effective way of helping children regulate their own behaviour.

Build self-esteem and your relationship While it is important to have strategies in place for misbehaviour, it is vitally important also to build children's self-esteem by praising good behaviour. So often children are ignored when they are behaving well, but praising them for being well behaved encourages them to do it again. Try to praise children at least five to ten times more than you would have to discipline them; consequences then have more impact. Having high self-esteem equips children in stressful situations, such as starting day care or being left with a new nanny, and makes them more likely to become happy, confident learners.

Protecting your child

Registered day-care facilities are expected to comply with local child protection procedures (approved by the Area Child Protection Committee) to ensure that all adults working with children are aware of signs and symptoms of different forms of abuse, and procedures to follow if they suspect a child is being harmed. You, too, need to be aware and be ready to act promptly if you notice the signs.

Types of abuse

Physical
May include punching, biting, hair pulling, kicking, burning and scalding, severe physical punishment, beating, whipping, slapping, hitting, shaking, drowning or suffocating.

Emotional
Persistent emotional ill treatment such as lack of praise, rejection, threatening and frightening behaviour, negative comparisons with others, belittling, name-

calling, shaming and humiliating, blaming, emotional degrading punishment such as tying to a chair.

Neglect
Persistent failure to provide physical, emotional and educational needs, such as lack of adequate care and supervision, abandoning, denial or delay of medical care, poor hygiene and witnessing abusive relationships.

Sexual
The involvement of developmentally immature children and adolescents in sexual activities that they do not truly comprehend, or which are illegal. They include contact such as rape and non-contact such as exposure to pornographic material or encouraging children to behave in inappropriate ways.

Signs to look for
If children are being abused in any way and whether in the home or outside they show signs in different ways. Here are some common symptoms:
- Aggression and anti-social behaviour.
- Hostility.
- Fear of adults or a particular person.
- Depression and a poor self-image.
- Apathy and lack of concentration.
- Inappropriate sexual awareness.
- Nightmares and bedwetting.
- Changes in appetite or general behaviour or demeanour.
- Returning home unclean and hungry.
- Being over-compliant and too keen to try to please you.

What to do
If you have any concerns about a child being abused, whether it is your child or not, it is your duty to report your concerns without delay to an appropriate authority who will advise you on what action they or you should take. This can include your social services department, the police, NSPCC, or other professional who is in touch with the child or family. Although it is rare, if you suspect that your child is in danger, keep him away from the childcare facility or carer, talk to the manager or carer and try to talk to your child.

Useful contacts

LOCAL CHILDCARE

ChildcareLink
08000 960 296
www.childcarelink.gov.uk

NACIS (National Association of Children's
Information Services)
020 7515 9000
www.nacis.org.uk

Sure Start
0870 000 2288
www.surestart.gov.uk

PARENTING ISSUES

NCB (National Children's Bureau)
020 7843 6000
www.ncb.org.uk

Parentline Plus
0808 800 222
www.parentline.org.uk

Fathers Direct
www.fathersdirect.com

Gingerbread (for lone families)
0800 018 4318
www.gingerbread.org.uk

FINANCES AND FLEXIBLE WORKING

Inland Revenue and Tax Credits helpline
0845 300 3900
www.inlandrevenue.gov.uk/taxcredits

Care to Learn?
0845 600 2809
www.dfes.gov.uk/caretolearn

Working families helpline
0800 013 0313
www.workingfamilies.org.uk

CARE FOR CHILDREN WITH SPECIAL NEEDS

Kids Active
020 7359 3635
www.kidsactive.org.uk

Disability Rights Commission
08457 622 633
www.drc-gb.org

Equal Opportunities Commission
08456 015 901
www.eoc.org.uk

CARE AT HOME

ANA (Association of Nanny Agencies)
www.anauk.org

International Nanny Association
www.nanny.org

National Childbirth Trust
0870 444 8707
www.nct-online.org

British High Commission/Home Office (au
pair scheme)
0870 606 7766
www.britishhighcommission.gov.uk
www.workingintheuk.gov.uk

The Disclosure Service (Criminal Records
Bureau)
0870 9090 811
www.disclosure.gov.uk

CARE OUTSIDE THE HOME

National Childminding Association
0800 169 4486
www.ncma.org.uk

Northern Ireland Childminding Association
028 9181 1015
www.nicma.org

Scottish Childminding Association
01786 445377
www.childminding.org

Wales PPA (Pre-school Playgroups
Association)
01686 624 573
www.walespa.org

NIPPA (The Early Years Organisation in
Northern Ireland)
028 25640111
www.nippa.org

National Day Nurseries Association
0870 774 4244
www.ndna.org.uk

Montessori Education UK
www.montessorieducationuk.org

PANN (Professional Association of Nursery
Nurses)
01322 372 337
www.pat.org.uk

SCHOOL-BASED CARE AND HOLIDAY CLUBS

4children (formerly Kid's Club Network)
020 7512 2112
www.4children.org.uk

CHILDCARER QUALIFICATIONS

QCA (Qualifications and Curriculum
Authority)
020 7509 5555
www.qca.org.uk

BTEC (Business and Technology Education
Council)
020 7393 4500
www.edexcel.org.uk

CACHE (Council for Awards in Children's
Care and Education)
01727 847 636
www.cache.org.uk

ACCAC (Qualifications, Curriculum and
Assessment Authority for Wales)
029 2037 5400
www.accac.org.uk

SNNB (Scottish Child Care and Education
Board)
6 Kilnford Crescent
Dundonald
Kilmnock
Ayrshire
KA2 9DW
(SAE required)

SQA (Scottish Qualifications Authority)
0141 242 2487
www.sqa.org.uk

CCA (Council for the Curriculum
Examinations and Assessment)
028 9026 1200
www.ccea.org.uk

REGISTRATION AND INSPECTION OF CHILDCARE

Ofsted (Office for Standards in Education)
0845 6014 771
0845 602 2260 for a copy of the National
Standards for under eights in England
www.ofsted.gov.uk

Childcare Approval Scheme
0845 7678 111
www.childcareapprovalscheme.co.uk

CSIW (Care Standards Inspectorate for Wales)
029 2047 8600
www.csiw.wales.gov.uk

SCRC (Scottish Commission for the
Regulation of Care)
01382 207 100
www.carecommission.com

Index

Acknowledgements

Executive Editor Jane McIntosh
Editor Alice Bowden
Executive Art Editor Geoff Fennell
Senior Production Controller Martin Croshaw